COURAGE ON THE BATTLEFIELD

TRUE STORIES OF SURVIVAL IN THE MILITARY

by Nel Yomtov

illustrated by Thomas Girard

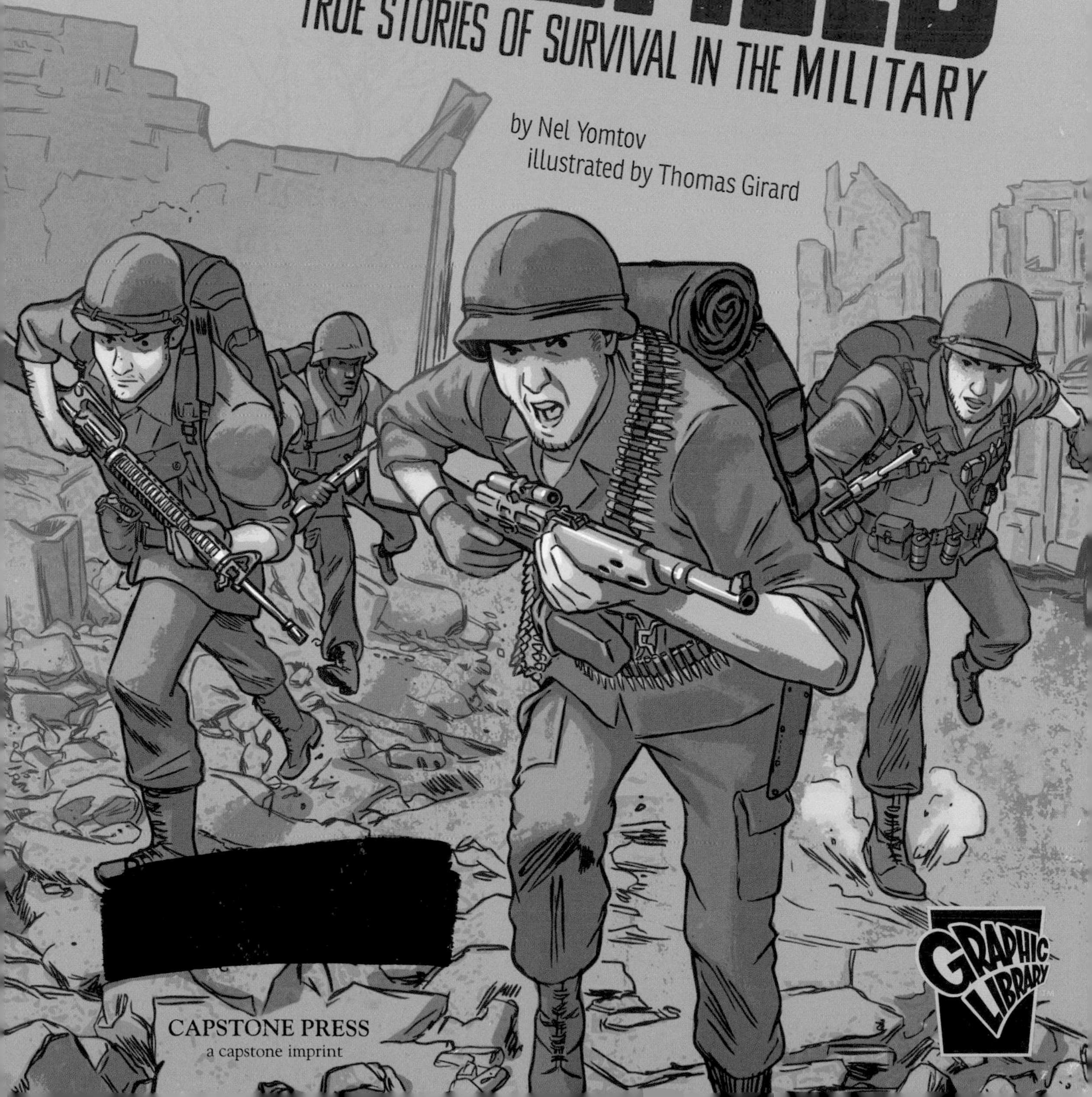

[redacted]

GRAPHIC LIBRARY

CAPSTONE PRESS
a capstone imprint

Graphic Library is published by Capstone Press,
1710 Roe Crest Drive, North Mankato, Minnesota 56003
www.capstonepub.com

Library of Congress Cataloging-in-Publication Data
Yomtov, Nelson.
  Courage on the battlefield : true stories of survival in the
military / by Nel Yomtov.
    pages cm.—(Graphic library. True stories of survival)
  Includes bibliographical references and index.
  Summary: "In graphic novel format, details true war
survival stories"—Provided by publisher.
  Audience: Grades 4-6.
  ISBN 978-1-4914-6571-4 (library binding)
  ISBN 978-1-4914-6575-2 (ebook pdf)
  1. Soldiers—United States—Comic books, strips, etc.—
Juvenile literature. 2. Combat survival—Comic books,
strips, etc.—Juvenile literature. I. Title. II. Title: True
tales of survival in the military.
  UA23.Y65 2014
  355.0092'273—dc23   2015001842

Editorial Credits:
Anthony Wacholtz, editor; Ashlee Suker, designer;
Nathan Gassman, creative director; Laura Manthe,
production specialist

Photo Credits:
Shutterstock: romanka, cover

FWINNG
FWINNG

Editor's note:
Direct quotations, noted in green type, appear on the
following pages:

  Page 7: John L. Ransom. *John Ransom's
    Andersonville Diary: Life Inside the Civil War's
    Most Infamous Prison*. New York: Berkley
    Books, 1986.

  Page 9: http://blogs.militarytimes.com/hall-of-valor/
    files/2012/02/amerine.pdf

  Page 23: http://www.americanvalor.net/heroes/332

  Page 25: Chris Ryan. *The One That Got Away*. Washington,
    D.C.: Potomac Books, 1998.

Printed in the United States of America
in North Mankato, Minnesota.
042015   008823CGF15

TABLE OF CONTENTS

THE WILL TO SURVIVE

You slowly and cautiously make your way through the rubble-filled street, taking cover behind anything you can. Suddenly, someone yells "Grenade!" and you dive behind a tank. The powerful explosion is deafening. You're unharmed, but a fellow soldier is hit hard by the blast. You rush to his aid, pulling him to safety as enemy bullets whiz past your head.

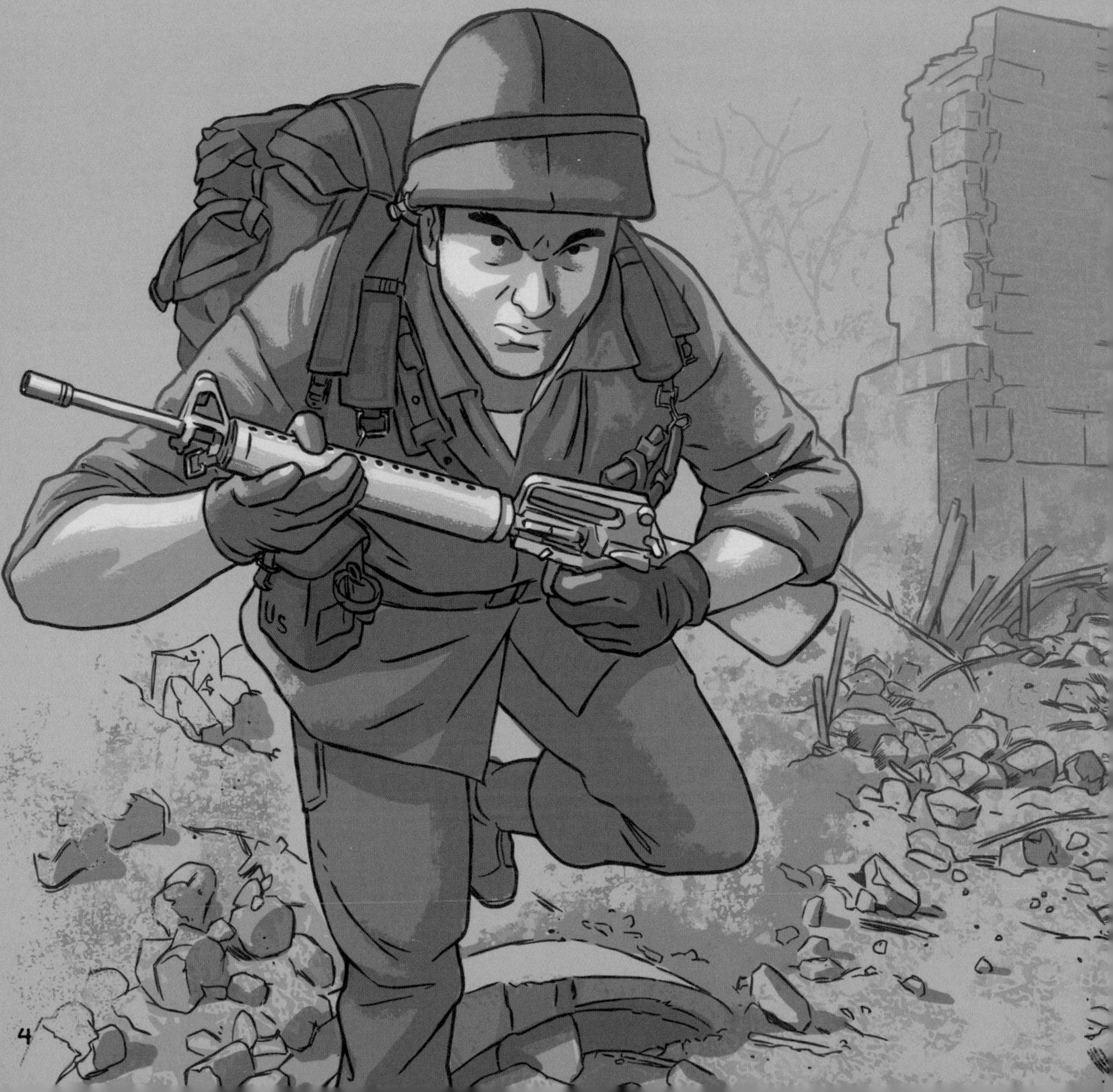
US

Combat soldiers have one of the most dangerous jobs in the world. They battle the enemy and face harsh conditions. Pain, fear, loneliness, stress, sorrow, thirst, and hunger are often part of their mission. Soldiers face their foes in blistering heat and bone-chilling temperatures. Injury—and death—hangs over every mission.

A soldier's goal is to survive and fight another day. Battling the enemy, and the elements of nature, tests a combat soldier's will to live. Life-threatening missions often stretch a warrior's mental and physical skills to their breaking points.

The soldiers you will meet in the following true tales of military survival bend. But they do not break.

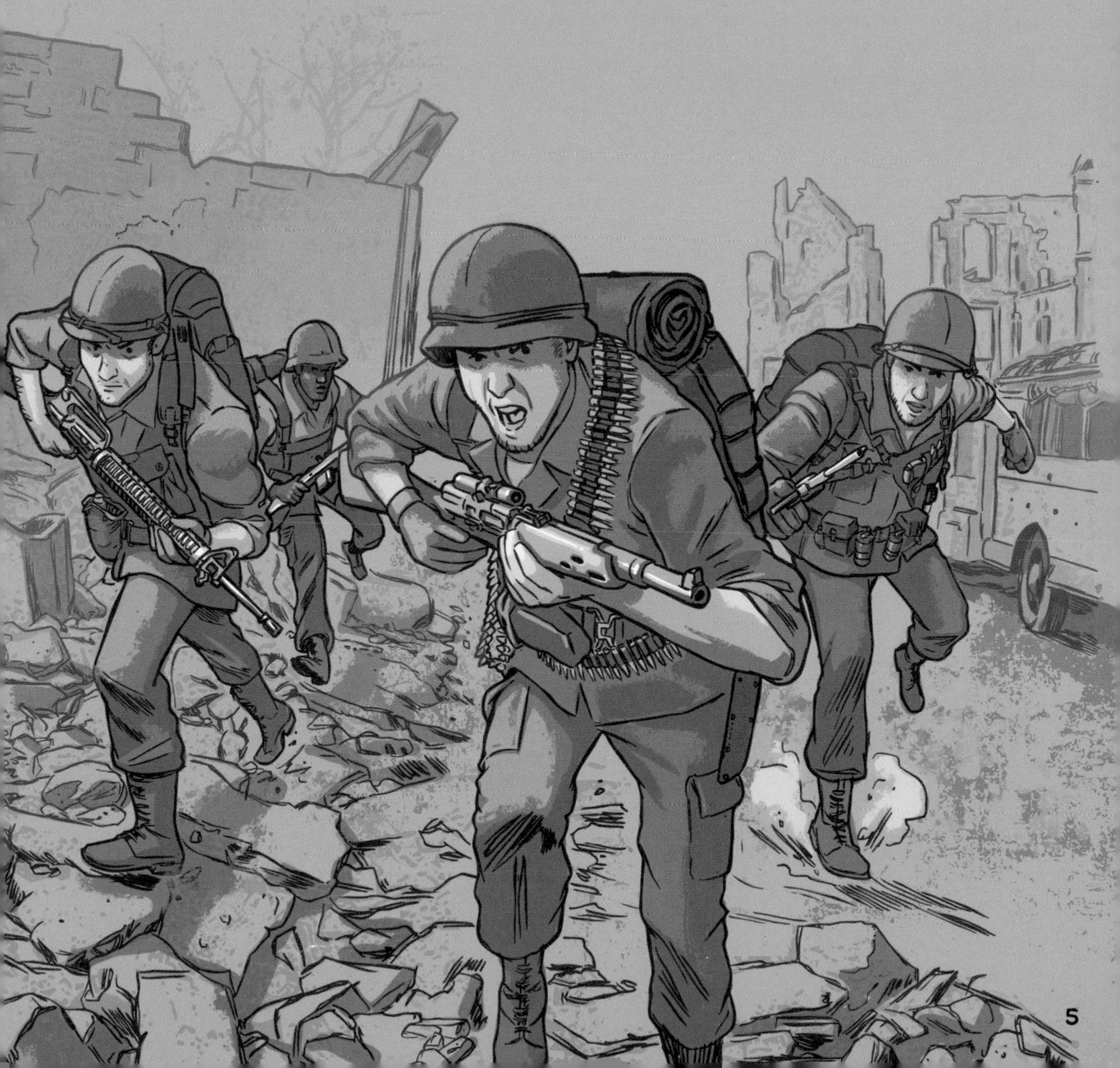

CHAPTER ONE

JOHN RANSOM
THE NIGHTMARE OF ANDERSONVILLE PRISON

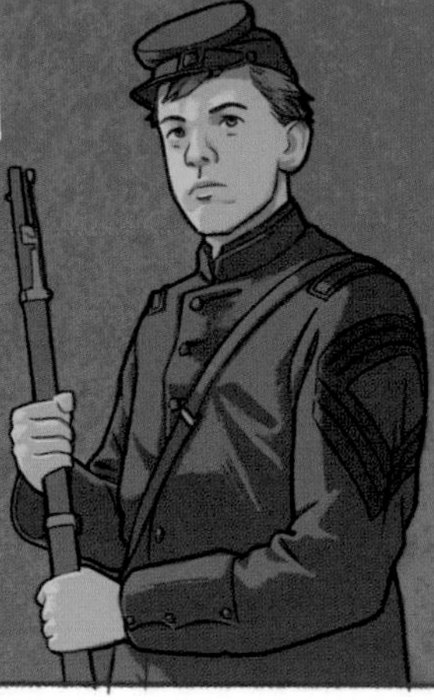

Twenty-year-old John Ransom was a sergeant in the 9th Michigan Calvary during the American Civil War (1861–1865). On November 6, 1863, he was captured by Confederate soldiers and sent to Belle Isle prison near Richmond, Virginia.

On March 14, 1864, Ransom arrived at the new prison at Andersonville, Georgia. He was held there until he was near death. Ransom never gave up hope—and he lived to tell his story.

Andersonville prison was built to house 10,000 Union prisoners. But at the height of its use, Ransom and nearly 33,000 prisoners were crammed into a tiny area covering 27 acres (11 hectares).

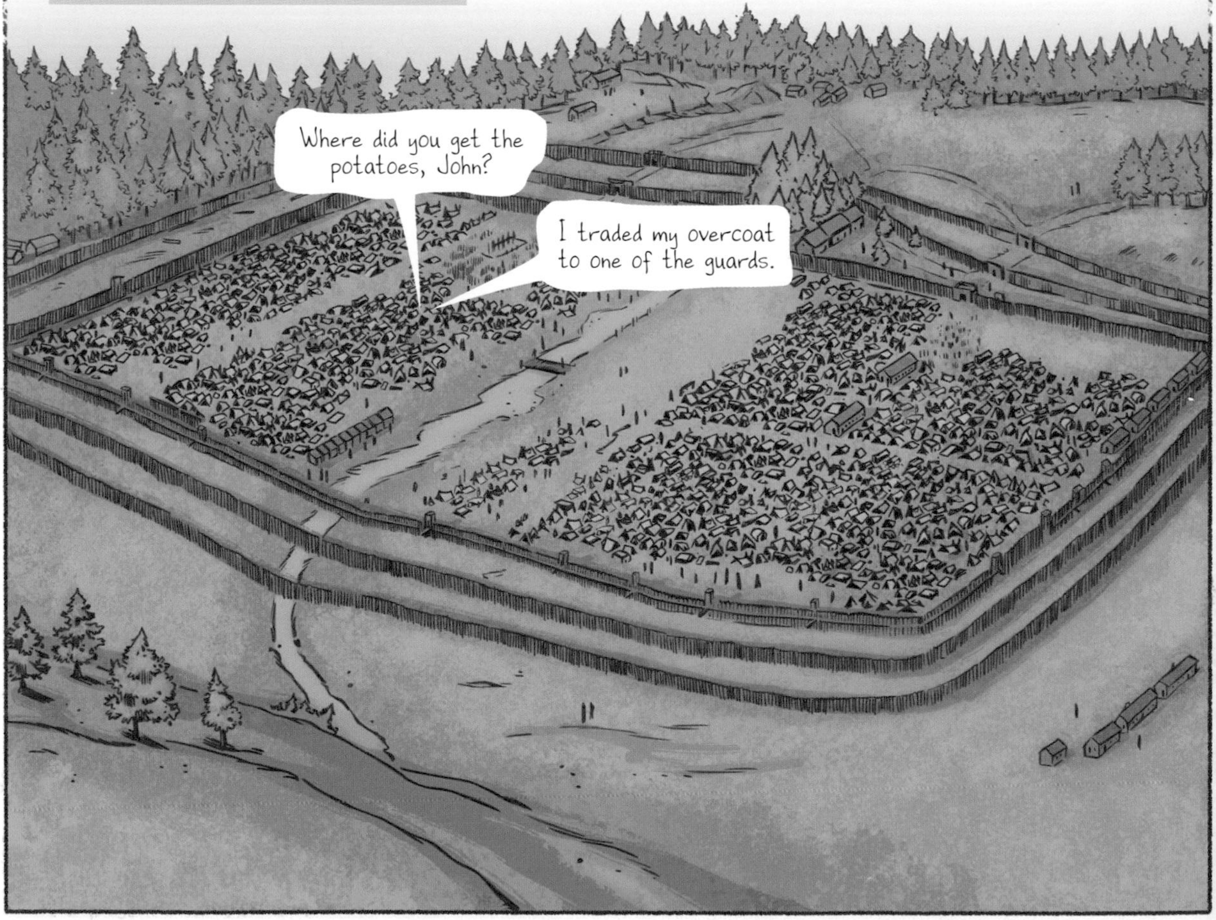
Where did you get the potatoes, John?
I traded my overcoat to one of the guards.

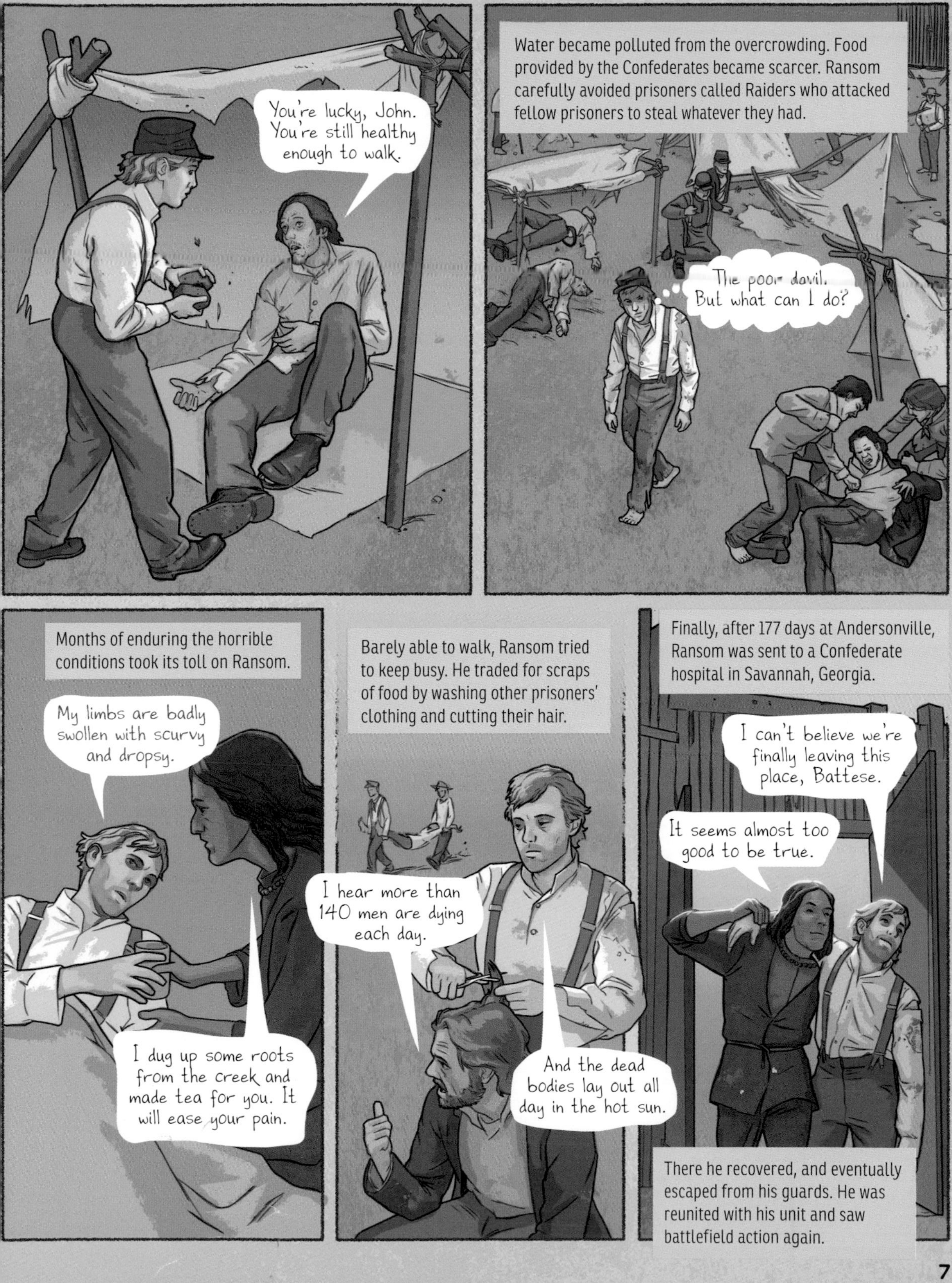
You're lucky, John. You're still healthy enough to walk.
Water became polluted from the overcrowding. Food provided by the Confederates became scarcer. Ransom carefully avoided prisoners called Raiders who attacked fellow prisoners to steal whatever they had.
The poor devil. But what can I do?
Months of enduring the horrible conditions took its toll on Ransom.
My limbs are badly swollen with scurvy and dropsy.
I dug up some roots from the creek and made tea for you. It will ease your pain.
Barely able to walk, Ransom tried to keep busy. He traded for scraps of food by washing other prisoners' clothing and cutting their hair.
I hear more than 140 men are dying each day.
And the dead bodies lay out all day in the hot sun.
Finally, after 177 days at Andersonville, Ransom was sent to a Confederate hospital in Savannah, Georgia.
I can't believe we're finally leaving this place, Battese.
It seems almost too good to be true.
There he recovered, and eventually escaped from his guards. He was reunited with his unit and saw battlefield action again.

CHAPTER TWO

RICHARD RONALD AMERINE
LOST IN THE JUNGLE

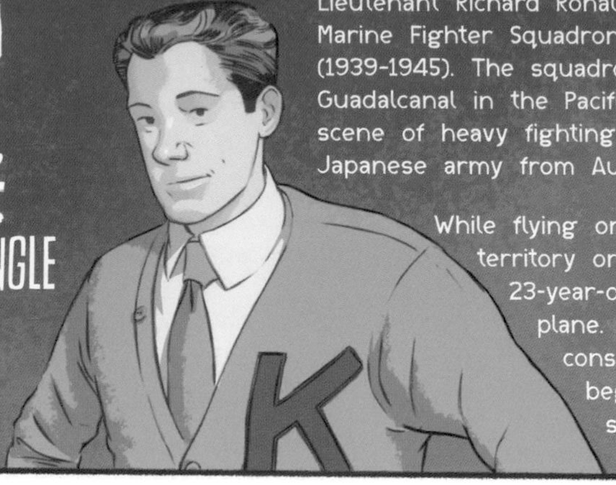

Lieutenant Richard Ronald Amerine was a pilot in Marine Fighter Squadron 224 during World War II (1939–1945). The squadron was based on the island of Guadalcanal in the Pacific Ocean. The island was the scene of heavy fighting between U.S. forces and the Japanese army from August 1942 to February 1943.

While flying on combat patrol over enemy territory on August 31, 1942, the 23-year-old pilot lost oxygen in his plane. He blacked out and lost consciousness. It was only the beginning of a heroic seven-day struggle to survive.

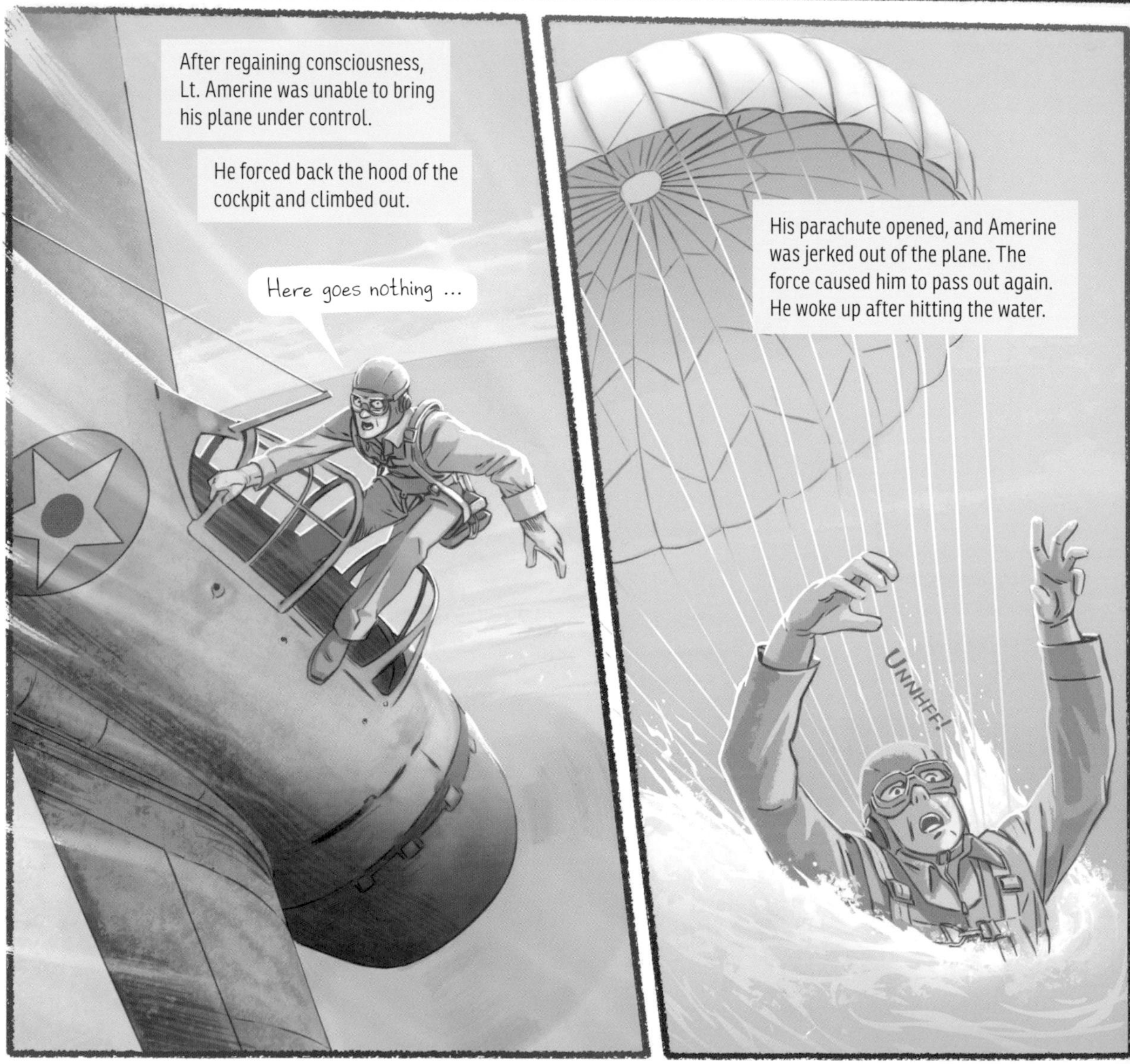
After regaining consciousness, Lt. Amerine was unable to bring his plane under control.
He forced back the hood of the cockpit and climbed out.
Here goes nothing ...
His parachute opened, and Amerine was jerked out of the plane. The force caused him to pass out again. He woke up after hitting the water.
UNNHFF!

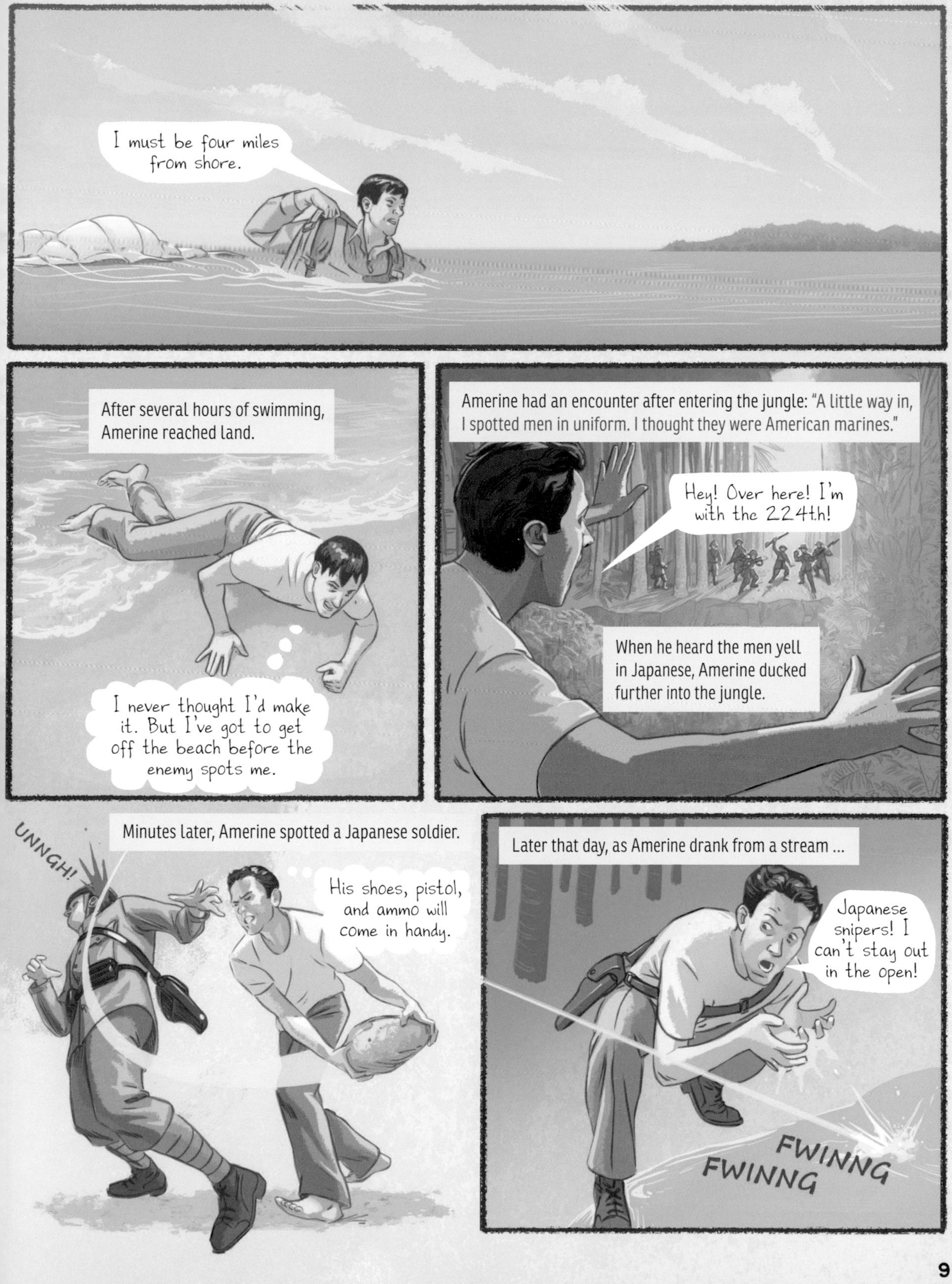
I must be four miles from shore.
After several hours of swimming, Amerine reached land.
I never thought I'd make it. But I've got to get off the beach before the enemy spots me.
Amerine had an encounter after entering the jungle: "A little way in, I spotted men in uniform. I thought they were American marines."
Hey! Over here! I'm with the 224th!
When he heard the men yell in Japanese, Amerine ducked further into the jungle.
Minutes later, Amerine spotted a Japanese soldier.
UNNGH!
His shoes, pistol, and ammo will come in handy.
Later that day, as Amerine drank from a stream ...
Japanese snipers! I can't stay out in the open!
FWINNG
FWINNG

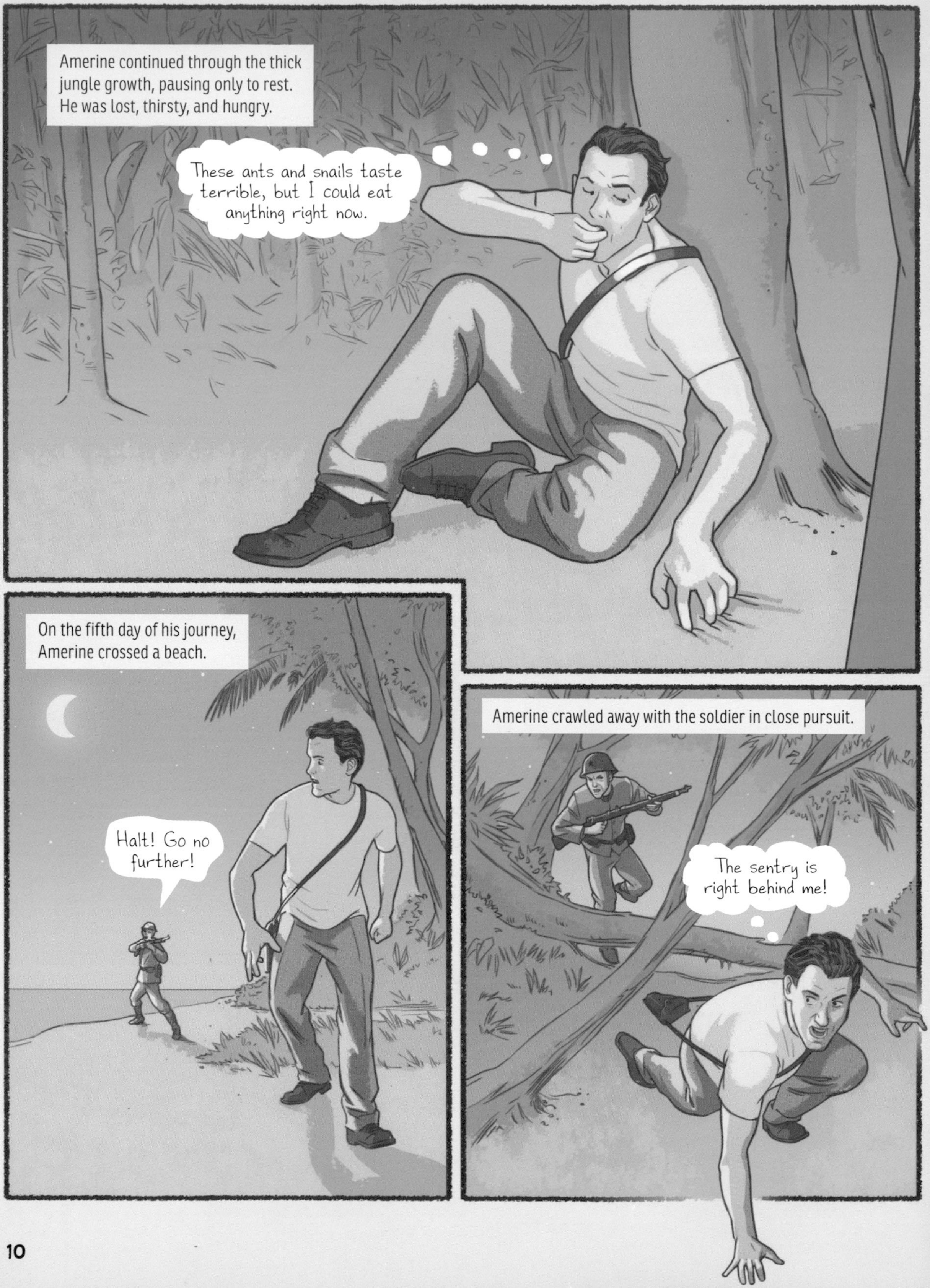
Amerine continued through the thick jungle growth, pausing only to rest. He was lost, thirsty, and hungry.
These ants and snails taste terrible, but I could eat anything right now.
On the fifth day of his journey, Amerine crossed a beach.
Halt! Go no further!
Amerine crawled away with the soldier in close pursuit.
The sentry is right behind me!

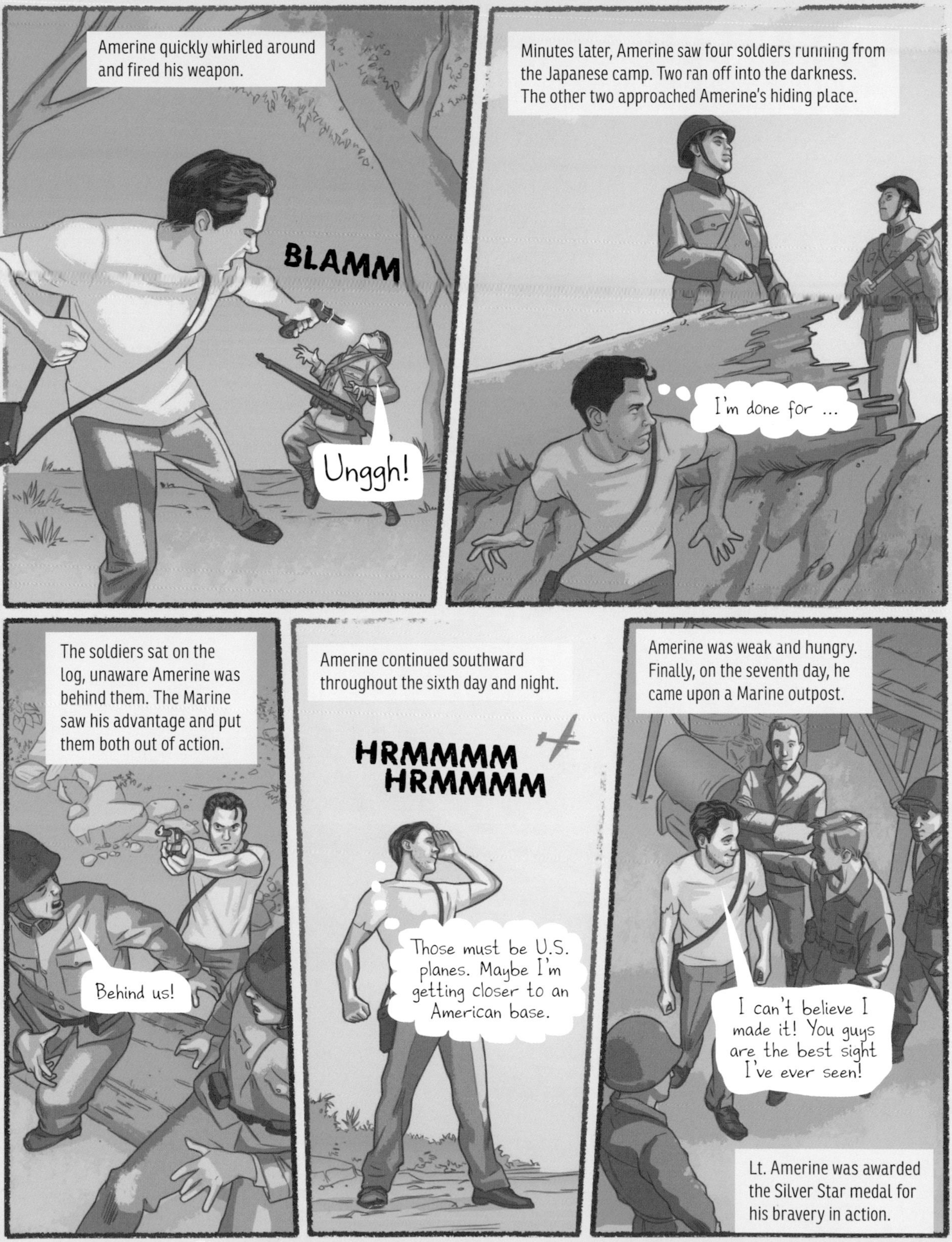
Amerine quickly whirled around and fired his weapon.
BLAMM
Unggh!
Minutes later, Amerine saw four soldiers running from the Japanese camp. Two ran off into the darkness. The other two approached Amerine's hiding place.
I'm done for ...
The soldiers sat on the log, unaware Amerine was behind them. The Marine saw his advantage and put them both out of action.
Behind us!
Amerine continued southward throughout the sixth day and night.
HRMMMM HRMMMM
Those must be U.S. planes. Maybe I'm getting closer to an American base.
Amerine was weak and hungry. Finally, on the seventh day, he came upon a Marine outpost.
I can't believe I made it! You guys are the best sight I've ever seen!
Lt. Amerine was awarded the Silver Star medal for his bravery in action.

CHAPTER THREE

JOHN BASILONE
LEGENDARY SURVIVOR AT GUADALCANAL

John Basilone was a U.S. Marine sergeant during World War II. In October 1942, he was stationed on the island of Guadalcanal in the Pacific Ocean. Weeks earlier, U.S. forces captured the island's airstrip, Henderson Field, from Japanese troops. Control of the airfield allowed the Americans to fly in supplies. The Japanese, however, wanted to regain the airfield. On one violent and bloody night, Sgt. Basilone did all he could to stand in their way.

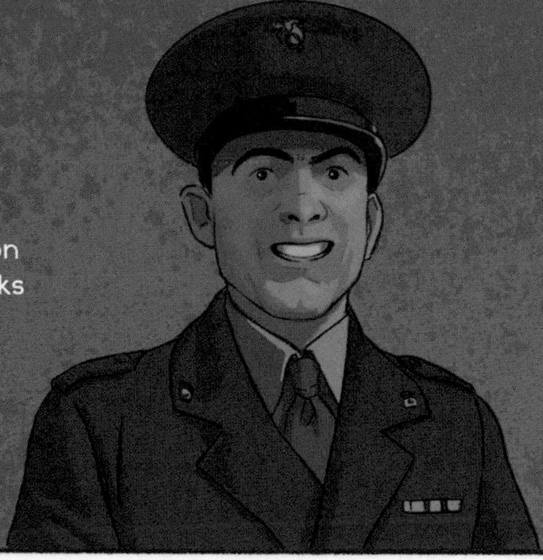

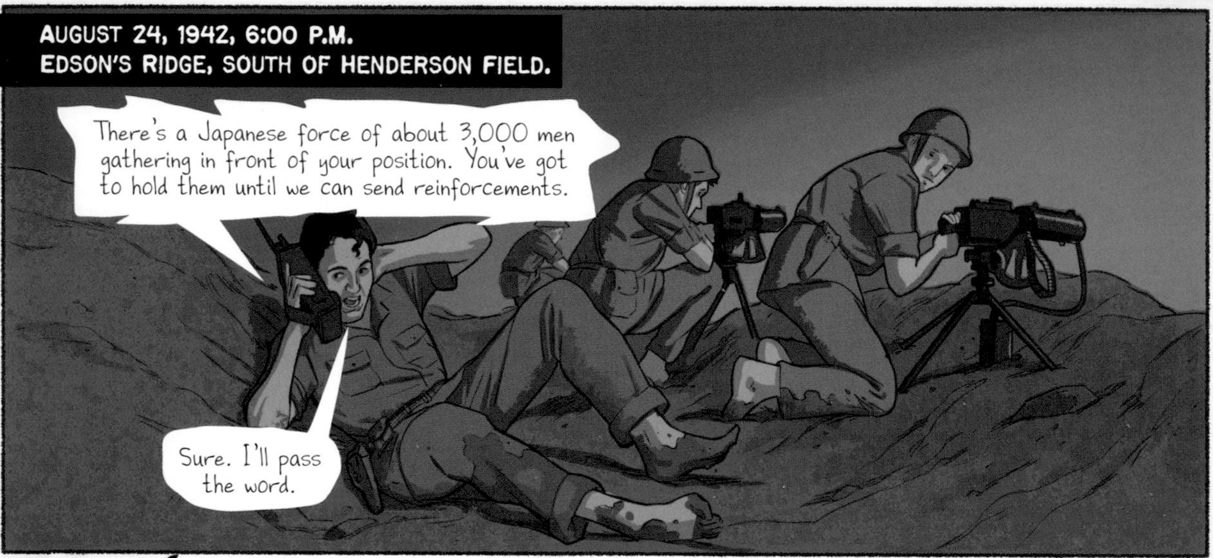
AUGUST 24, 1942, 6:00 P.M.
EDSON'S RIDGE, SOUTH OF HENDERSON FIELD.
There's a Japanese force of about 3,000 men gathering in front of your position. You've got to hold them until we can send reinforcements.
Sure. I'll pass the word.

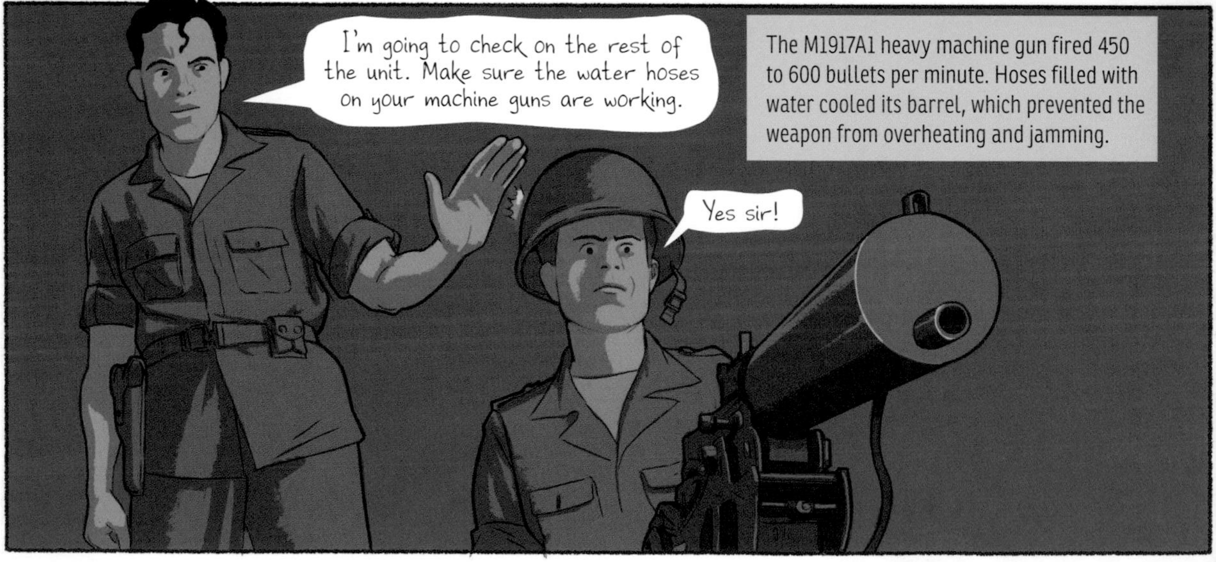
I'm going to check on the rest of the unit. Make sure the water hoses on your machine guns are working.
The M1917A1 heavy machine gun fired 450 to 600 bullets per minute. Hoses filled with water cooled its barrel, which prevented the weapon from overheating and jamming.
Yes sir!

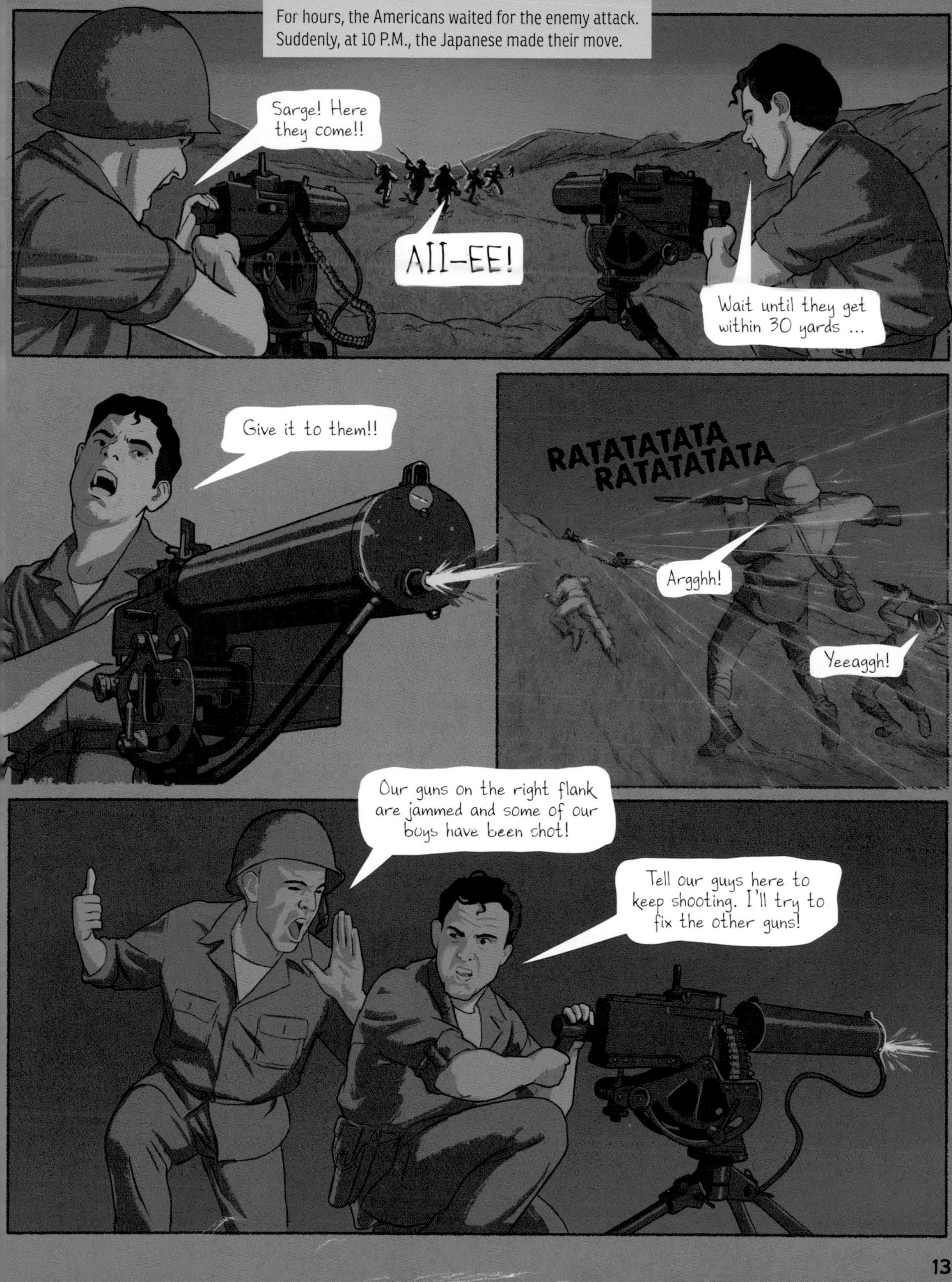
For hours, the Americans waited for the enemy attack. Suddenly, at 10 P.M., the Japanese made their move.
Sarge! Here they come!!
AII-EE!
Wait until they get within 30 yards ...
Give it to them!!
RATATATATA RATATATATA
Argghh!
Yeeaggh!
Our guns on the right flank are jammed and some of our boys have been shot!
Tell our guys here to keep shooting. I'll try to fix the other guns!

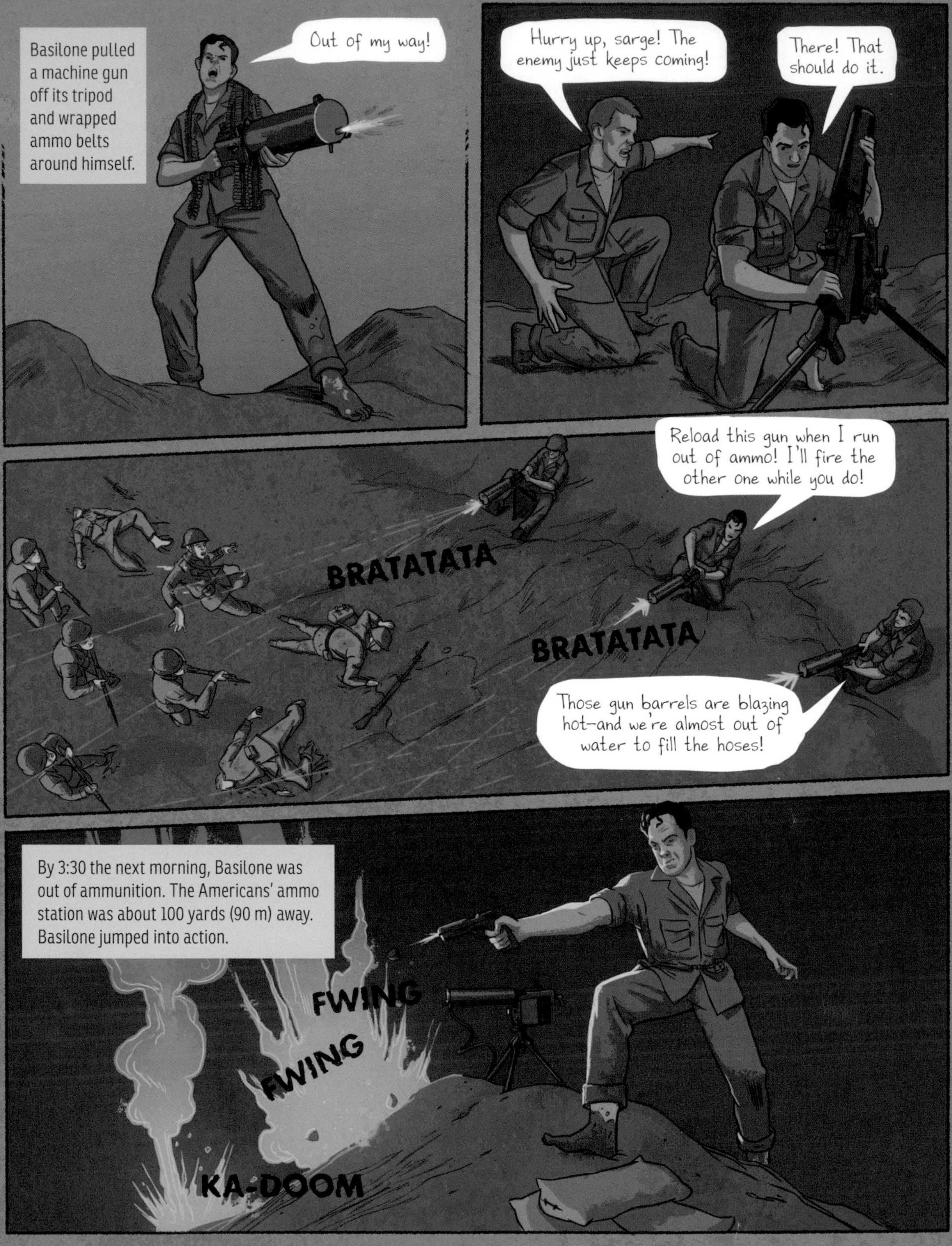
Basilone pulled a machine gun off its tripod and wrapped ammo belts around himself.
Out of my way!
Hurry up, sarge! The enemy just keeps coming!
There! That should do it.
Reload this gun when I run out of ammo! I'll fire the other one while you do!
BRATATATA
BRATATATA
Those gun barrels are blazing hot—and we're almost out of water to fill the hoses!
By 3:30 the next morning, Basilone was out of ammunition. The Americans' ammo station was about 100 yards (90 m) away. Basilone jumped into action.
FWING
FWING
KA-DOOM

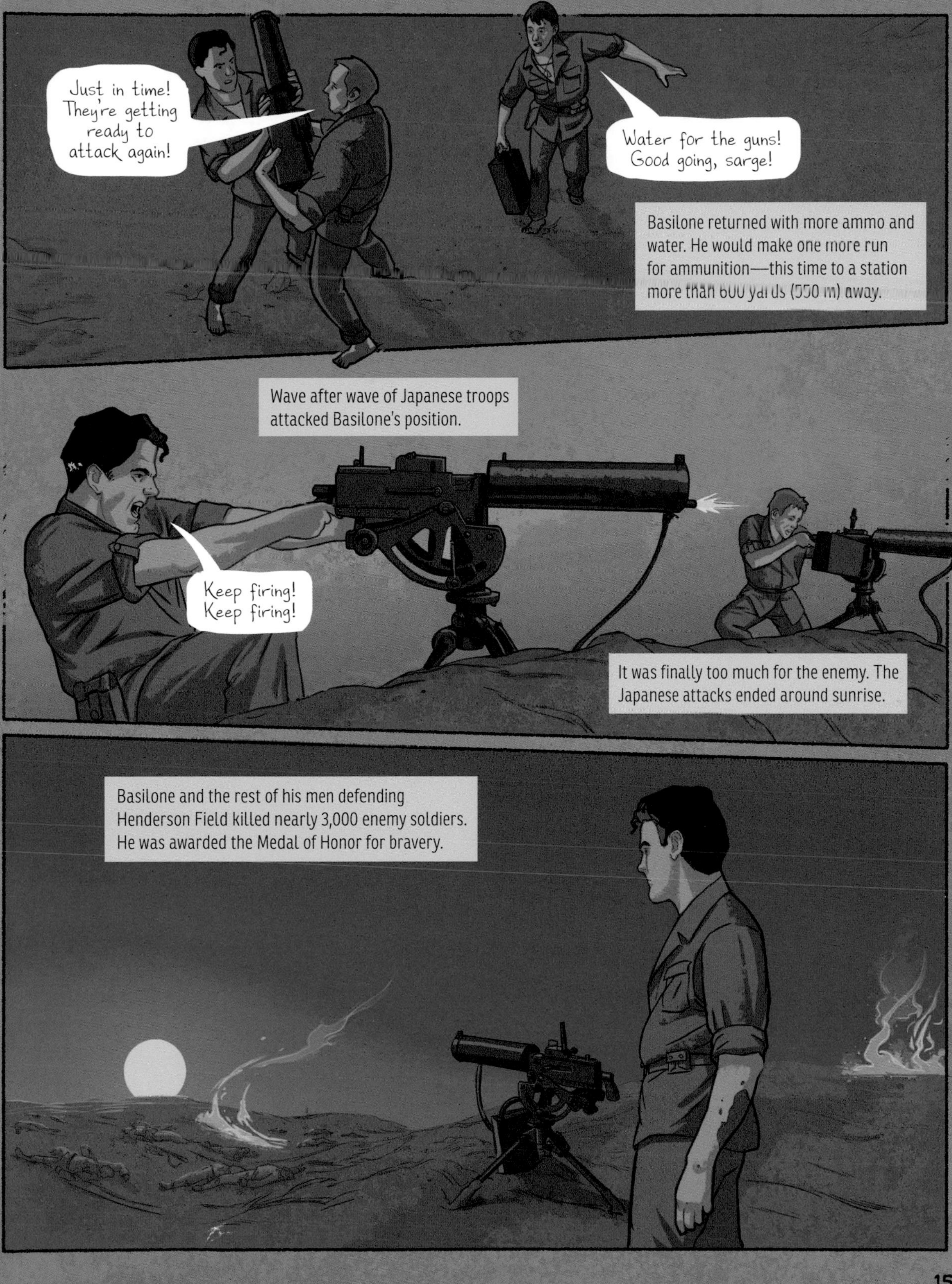
Just in time! They're getting ready to attack again!
Water for the guns! Good going, sarge!
Basilone returned with more ammo and water. He would make one more run for ammunition—this time to a station more than 600 yards (550 m) away.
Wave after wave of Japanese troops attacked Basilone's position.
Keep firing! Keep firing!
It was finally too much for the enemy. The Japanese attacks ended around sunrise.
Basilone and the rest of his men defending Henderson Field killed nearly 3,000 enemy soldiers. He was awarded the Medal of Honor for bravery.

CHAPTER FOUR

JOHN LEE LEVITOW
GUNSHIP HERO IN VIETNAM

Airman First Class John Lee Levitow was a loadmaster serving in the U.S. Air Force during the Vietnam War (1955-1975). On February 24, 1969, he flew aboard an AC-47 "Spooky" gunship over the jungles of South Vietnam. Levitow's job was to set up the flares and pass them to the gunner. The gunner would toss the tubes out the cargo door to light up the skies and the battlefield for American troops fighting on the ground. It had been a busy evening, but then disaster struck.

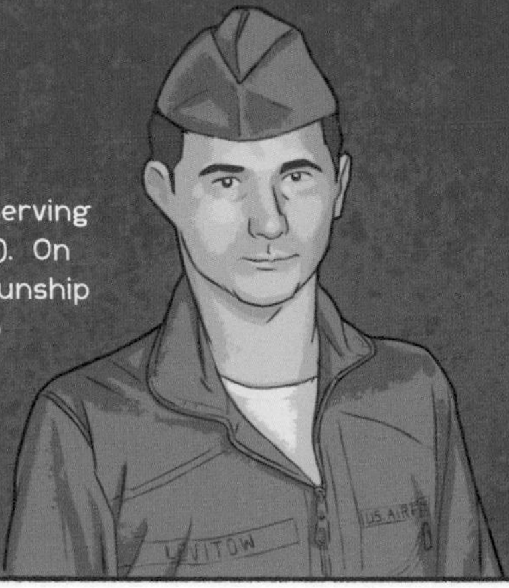
LEVITOW
U.S. AIR

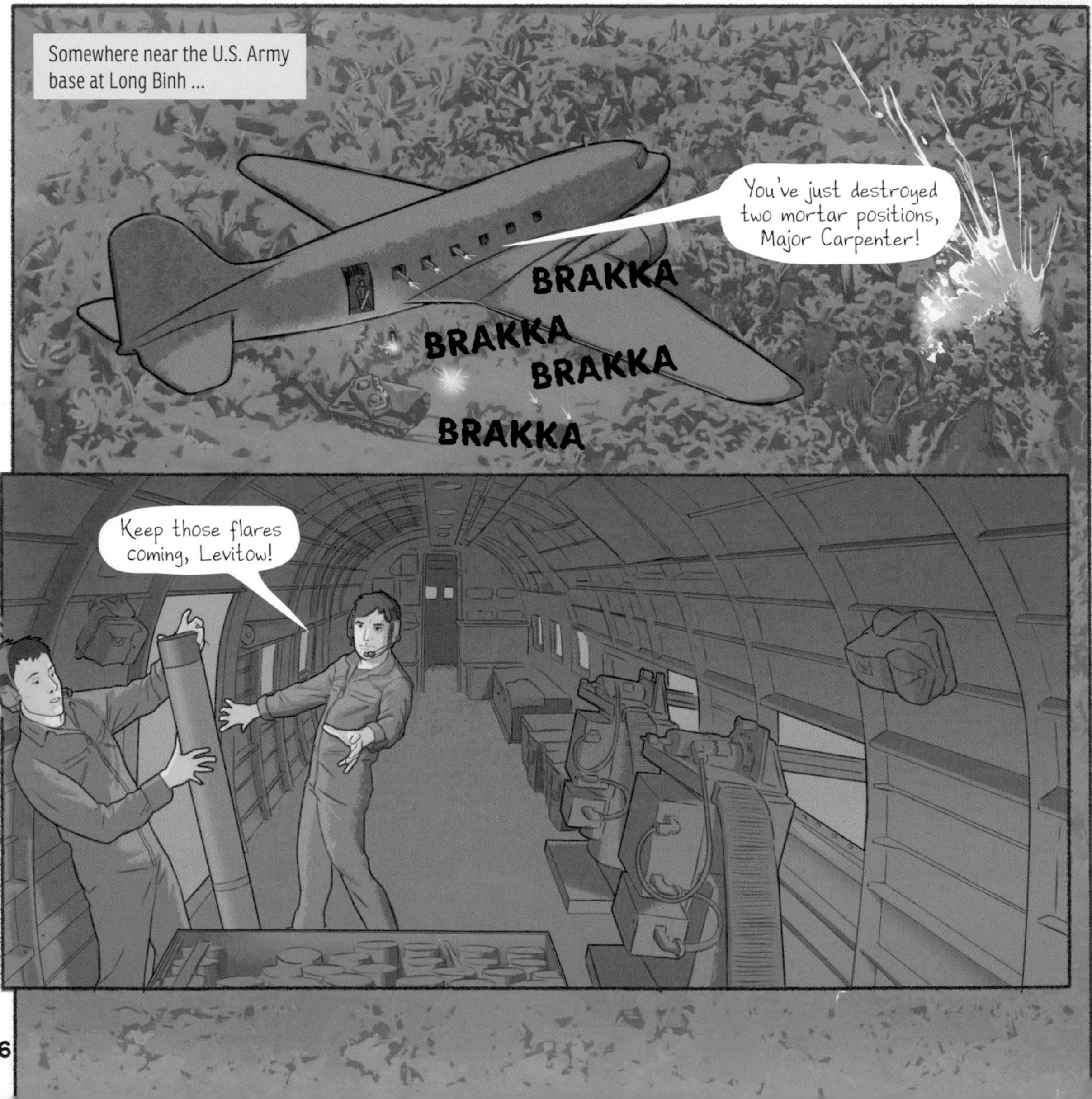
Somewhere near the U.S. Army base at Long Binh ...
You've just destroyed two mortar positions, Major Carpenter!
BRAKKA
BRAKKA
BRAKKA
BRAKKA
Keep those flares coming, Levitow!

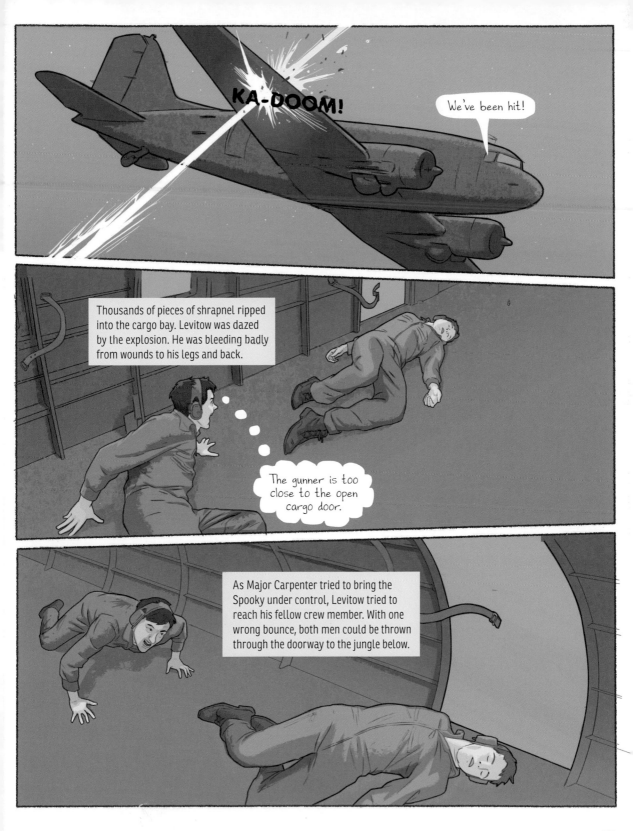

KA-DOOM!

We've been hit!

Thousands of pieces of shrapnel ripped into the cargo bay. Levitow was dazed by the explosion. He was bleeding badly from wounds to his legs and back.

The gunner is too close to the open cargo door.

As Major Carpenter tried to bring the Spooky under control, Levitow tried to reach his fellow crew member. With one wrong bounce, both men could be thrown through the doorway to the jungle below.

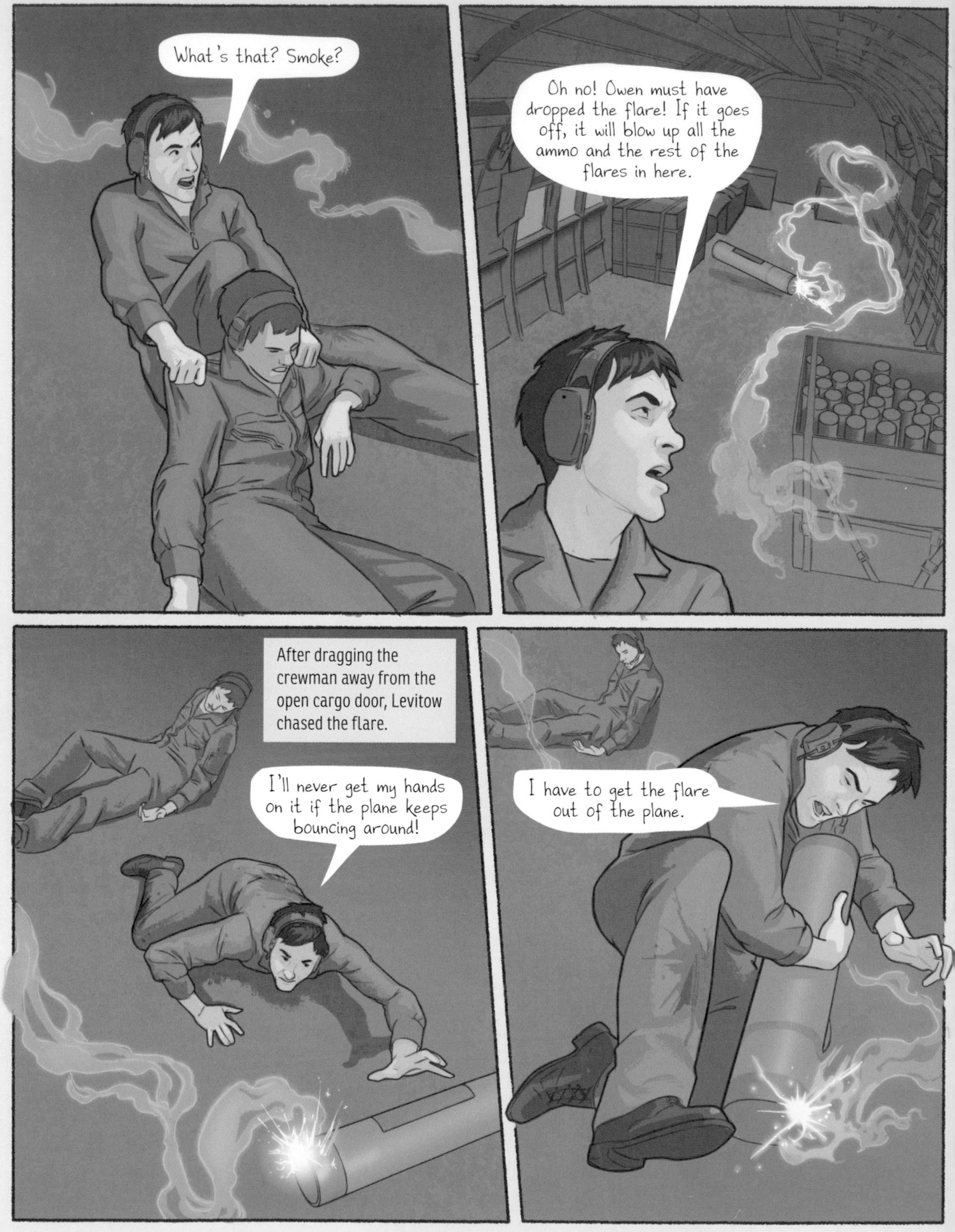
What's that? Smoke?
Oh no! Owen must have dropped the flare! If it goes off, it will blow up all the ammo and the rest of the flares in here.
After dragging the crewman away from the open cargo door, Levitow chased the flare.
I'll never get my hands on it if the plane keeps bouncing around!
I have to get the flare out of the plane.

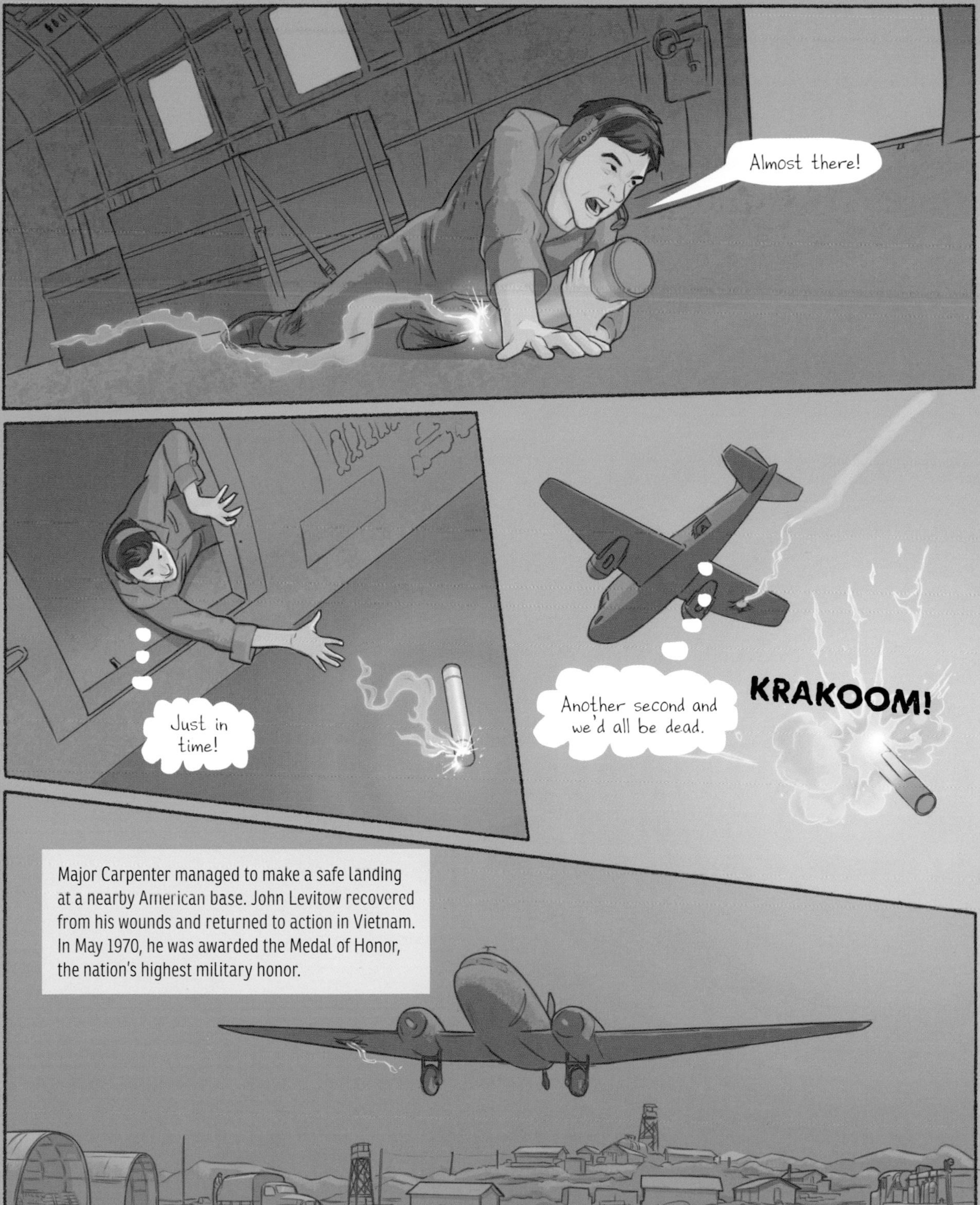
Almost there!
Just in time!
Another second and we'd all be dead.
KRAKOOM!
Major Carpenter managed to make a safe landing at a nearby American base. John Levitow recovered from his wounds and returned to action in Vietnam. In May 1970, he was awarded the Medal of Honor, the nation's highest military honor.

CHAPTER FIVE

CHRIS RYAN
THE SAGA OF BRAVO TWO ZERO

Chris Ryan was a corporal in the British Special Air Service (SAS) during the First Gulf War (1990-1991) in 1991. Ryan's 8-man patrol was called Bravo Two Zero. Part of its mission was to locate mobile enemy missile launchers within Iraq and call for air attacks to destroy them.

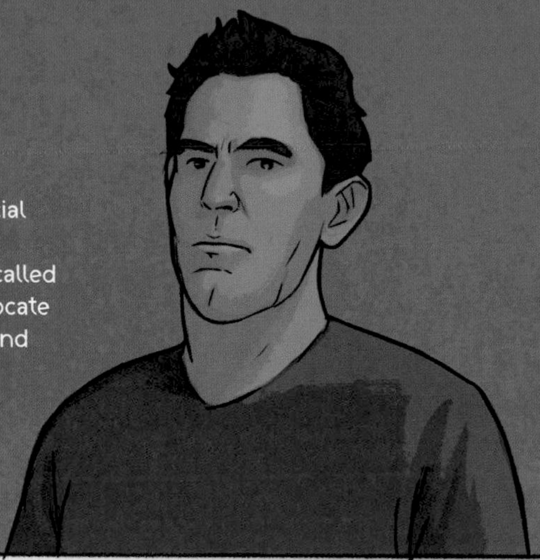

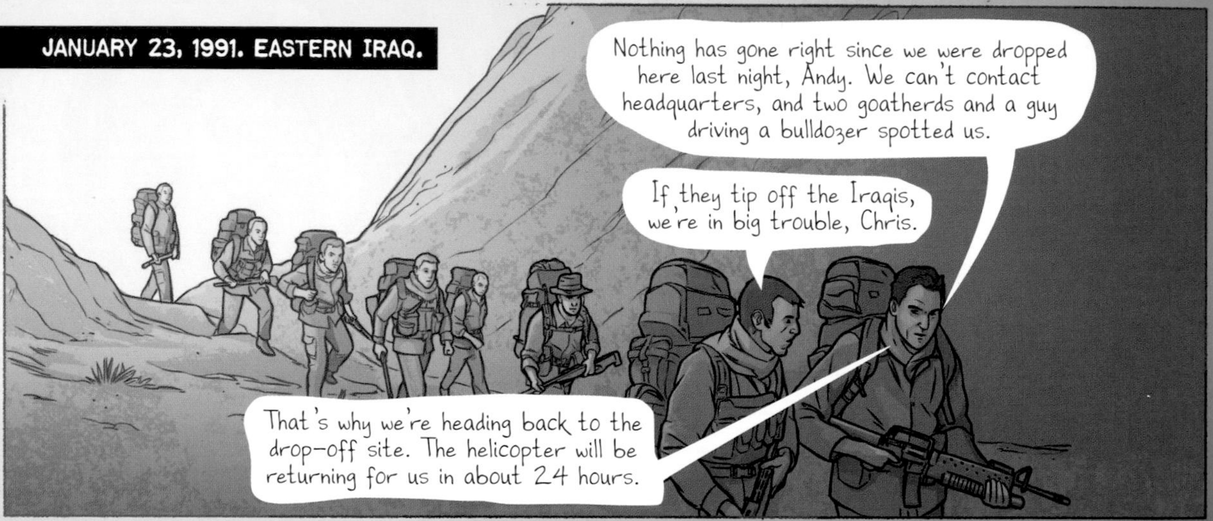

JANUARY 23, 1991. EASTERN IRAQ.
Nothing has gone right since we were dropped here last night, Andy. We can't contact headquarters, and two goatherds and a guy driving a bulldozer spotted us.
If they tip off the Iraqis, we're in big trouble, Chris.
That's why we're heading back to the drop-off site. The helicopter will be returning for us in about 24 hours.

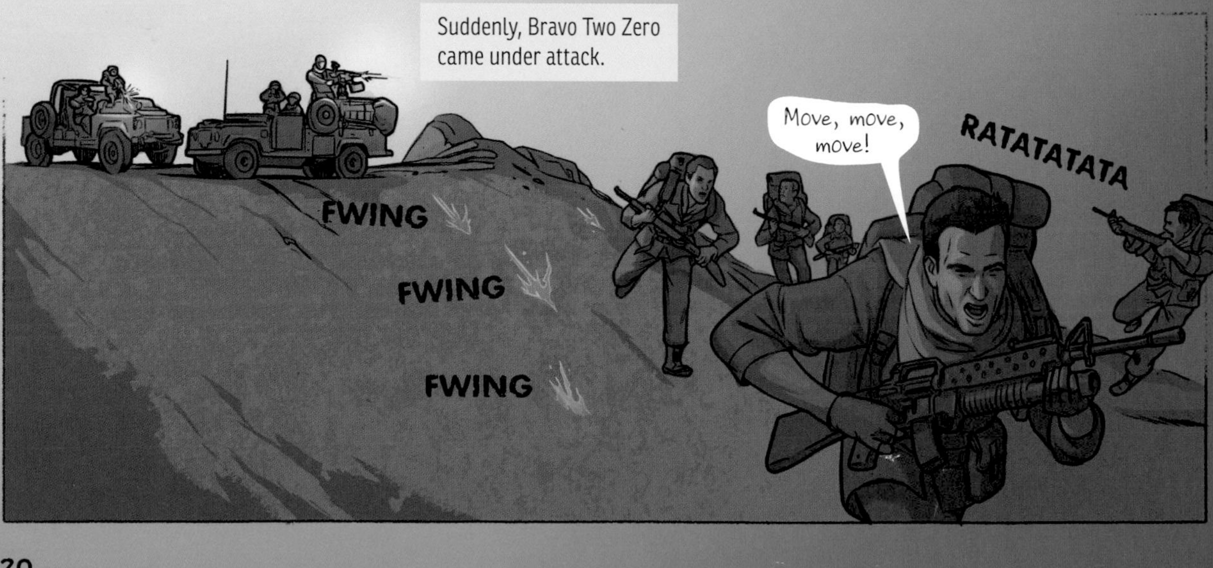

Suddenly, Bravo Two Zero came under attack.
Move, move, move!
RATATATATA
FWING
FWING
FWING

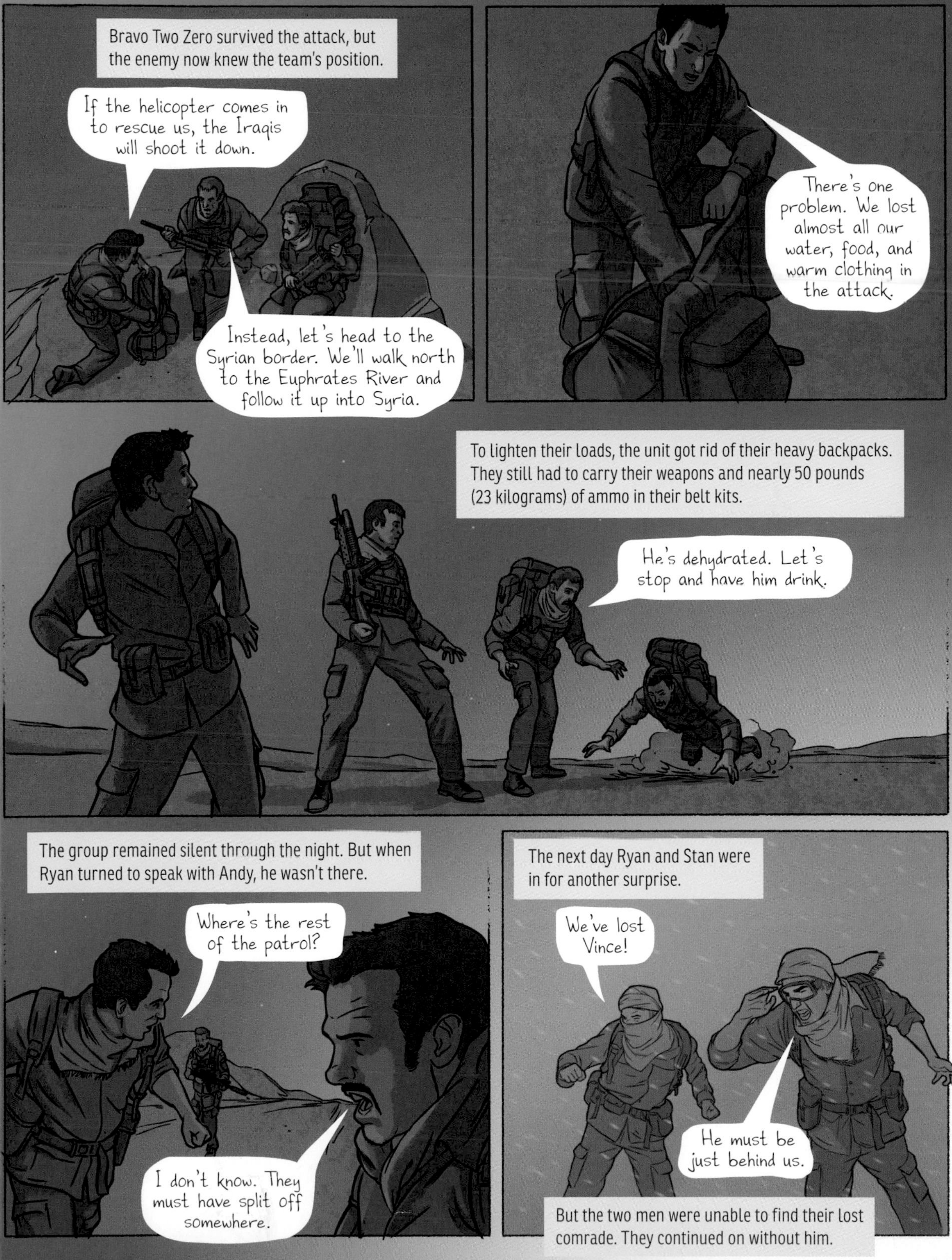
Bravo Two Zero survived the attack, but the enemy now knew the team's position.
If the helicopter comes in to rescue us, the Iraqis will shoot it down.
Instead, let's head to the Syrian border. We'll walk north to the Euphrates River and follow it up into Syria.
There's one problem. We lost almost all our water, food, and warm clothing in the attack.
To lighten their loads, the unit got rid of their heavy backpacks. They still had to carry their weapons and nearly 50 pounds (23 kilograms) of ammo in their belt kits.
He's dehydrated. Let's stop and have him drink.
The group remained silent through the night. But when Ryan turned to speak with Andy, he wasn't there.
Where's the rest of the patrol?
I don't know. They must have split off somewhere.
The next day Ryan and Stan were in for another surprise.
We've lost Vince!
He must be just behind us.
But the two men were unable to find their lost comrade. They continued on without him.

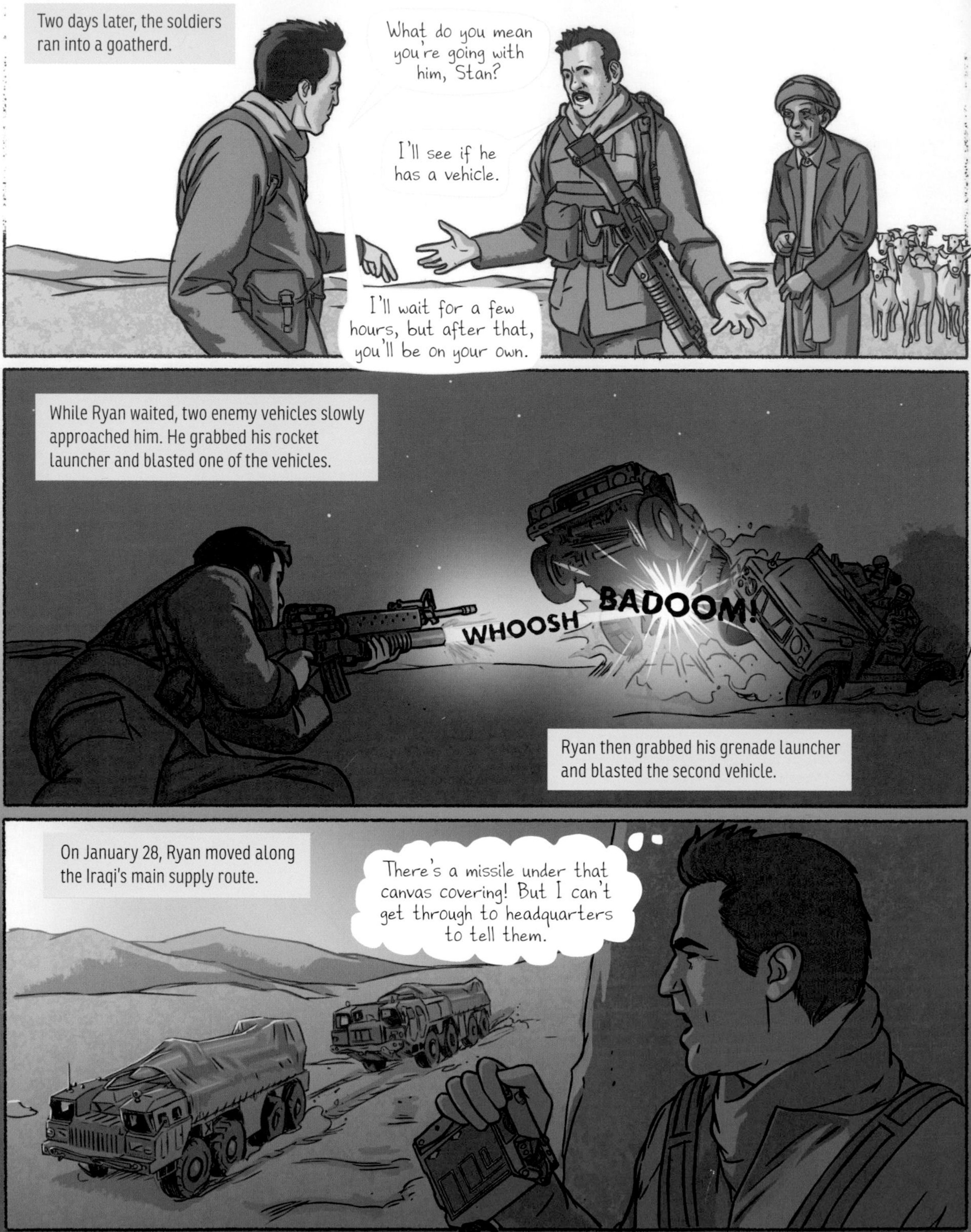

Two days later, the soldiers ran into a goatherd.
What do you mean you're going with him, Stan?
I'll see if he has a vehicle.
I'll wait for a few hours, but after that, you'll be on your own.
While Ryan waited, two enemy vehicles slowly approached him. He grabbed his rocket launcher and blasted one of the vehicles.
WHOOSH
BADOOM!
Ryan then grabbed his grenade launcher and blasted the second vehicle.
On January 28, Ryan moved along the Iraqi's main supply route.
There's a missile under that canvas covering! But I can't get through to headquarters to tell them.

The next day, Ryan hid in a drainpipe. He drank water he had gotten from a stream sometime earlier.

THBBBPT!!

Ryan later learned the water was contaminated with nuclear waste.

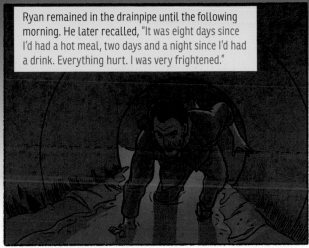

Ryan remained in the drainpipe until the following morning. He later recalled, "It was eight days since I'd had a hot meal, two days and a night since I'd had a drink. Everything hurt. I was very frightened."

Ryan soon approached what he believed was the Syria-Iraq border.

This doesn't look like much of a border. Maybe it's a fake one. I'll keeping moving on.

The next morning, Ryan came upon a barn.

Syria? Is this Syria?

Yes, yes Syria.

Syrian police arranged for Ryan's safe flight back to SAS headquarters in Saudi Arabia. His 190-mile (306-kilometer), 8-day ordeal was over. Three members of Bravo Two Zero, however, died on the mission. Ryan was awarded Britain's Military Medal for his actions.

CHAPTER SIX

KIM CAMPBELL

UNDER FIRE IN IRAQ

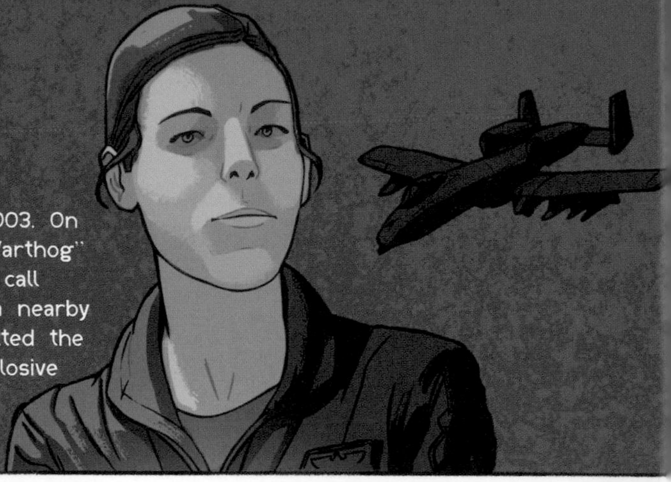

Captain Kim Campbell was a pilot during Operation Iraqi Freedom (2003-2010) in 2003. On April 7, 2003, she was flying her A-10 "Warthog" Thunderbolt II jet over Baghdad, Iraq. A call came over her radio that U.S. troops at a nearby bridge were under attack. When she spotted the fighting, she fired the Warthog's high-explosive rockets at Iraqi Republican Guard troops. Campbell's troubles began moments later.

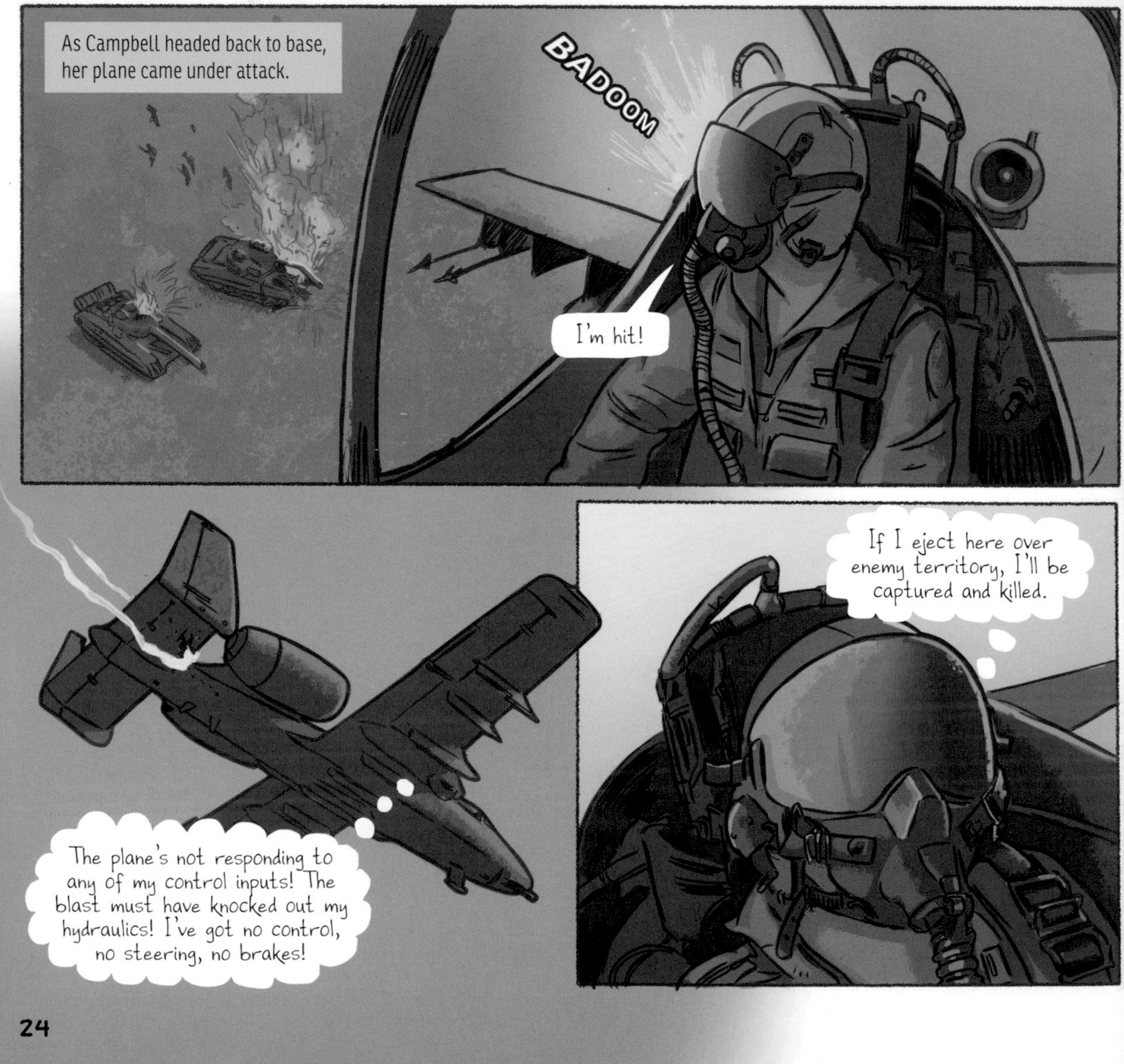
As Campbell headed back to base, her plane came under attack.
BADOOM
I'm hit!
The plane's not responding to any of my control inputs! The blast must have knocked out my hydraulics! I've got no control, no steering, no brakes!
If I eject here over enemy territory, I'll be captured and killed.

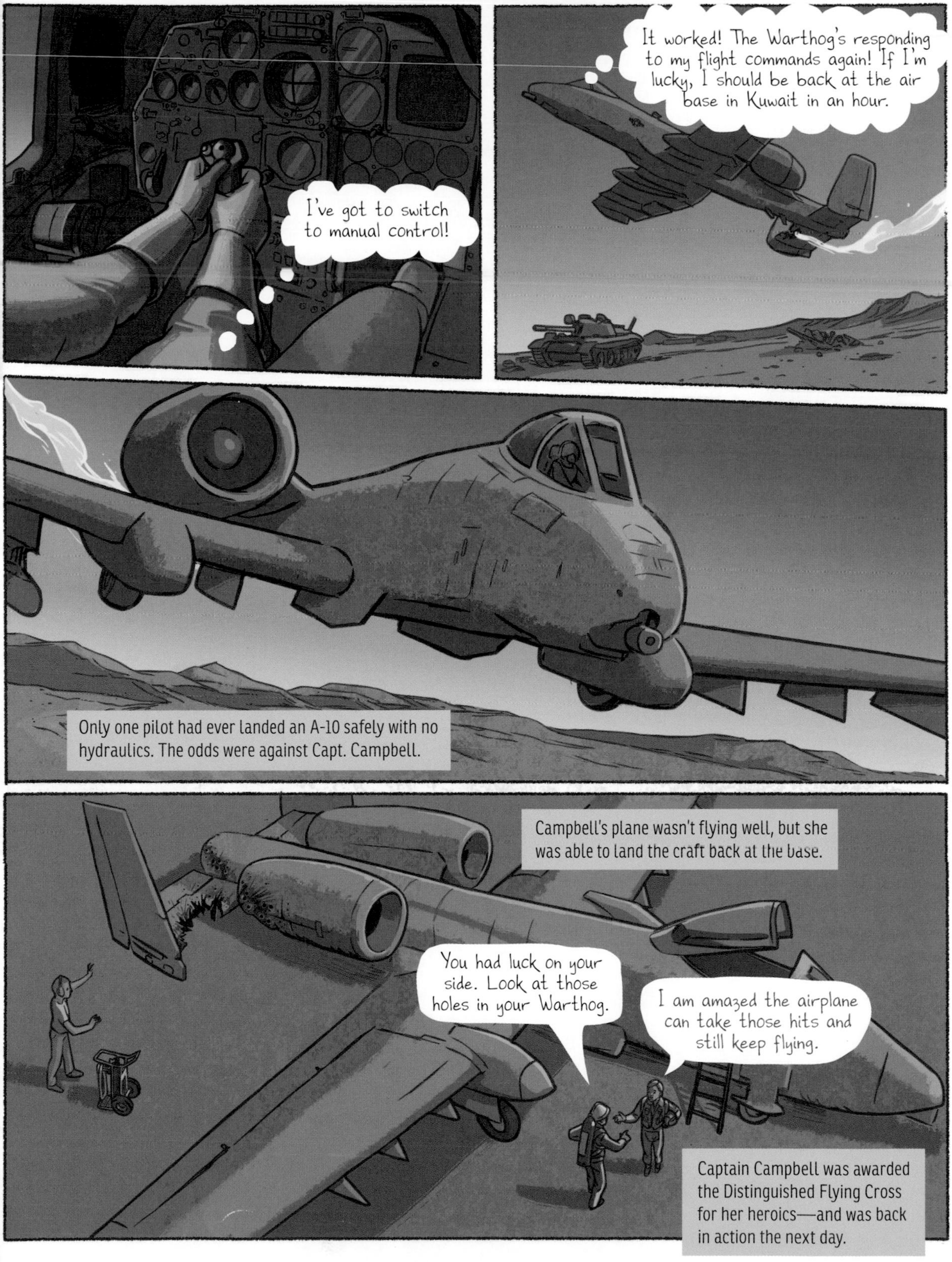
I've got to switch to manual control!
It worked! The Warthog's responding to my flight commands again! If I'm lucky, I should be back at the air base in Kuwait in an hour.
Only one pilot had ever landed an A-10 safely with no hydraulics. The odds were against Capt. Campbell.
Campbell's plane wasn't flying well, but she was able to land the craft back at the base.
You had luck on your side. Look at those holes in your Warthog.
I am amazed the airplane can take those hits and still keep flying.
Captain Campbell was awarded the Distinguished Flying Cross for her heroics—and was back in action the next day.

CHAPTER SEVEN

MARCUS LUTTRELL
NAVY SEAL TRAPPED IN AFGHANISTAN

Marcus Luttrell was a Second Class Hospital Corpsman who served in a U.S. Navy SEAL (Sea, Air, Land) team during the war in Afghanistan (2001-2014). On the night of June 27, 2005, Luttrell and three fellow SEALs were dropped by helicopters into a remote mountainous region of eastern Afghanistan. Their mission was to capture or kill Ahmad Shah. He was the leader of Taliban forces responsible for several deadly attacks on U.S. Marines.

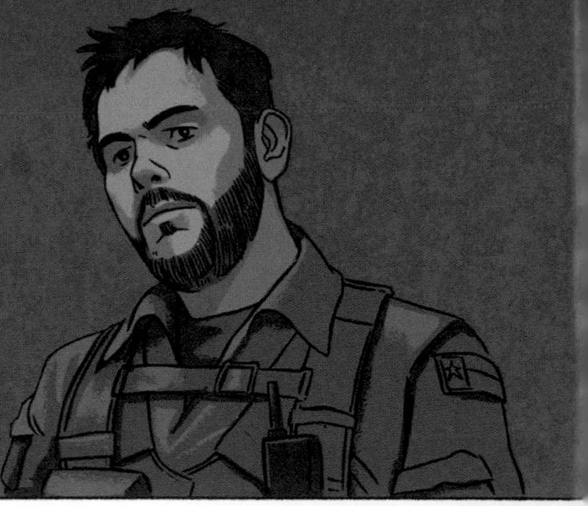

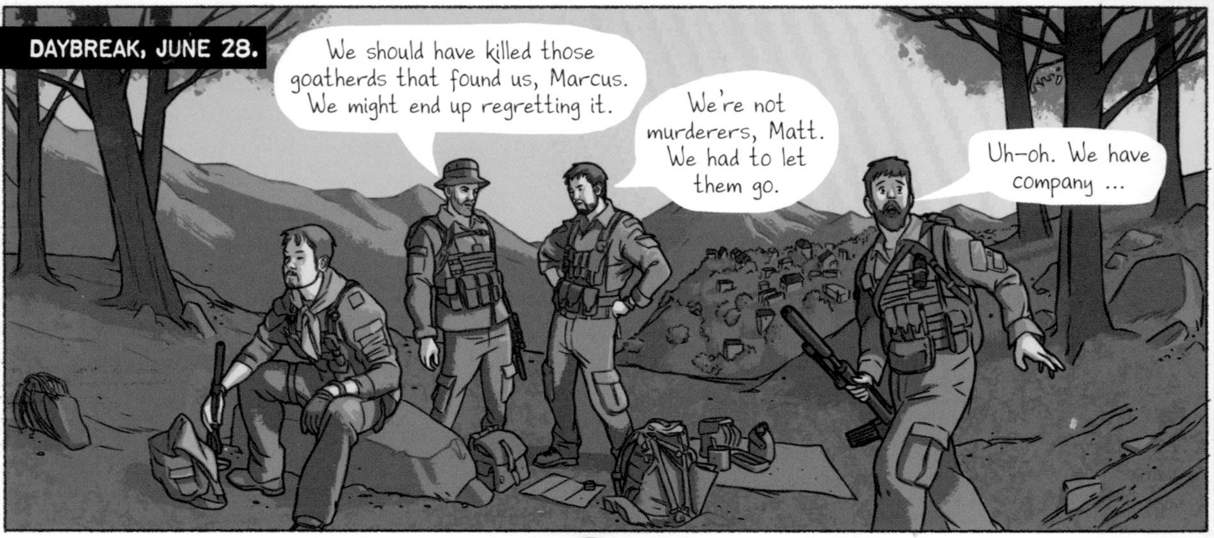
DAYBREAK, JUNE 28.
We should have killed those goatherds that found us, Marcus. We might end up regretting it.
We're not murderers, Matt. We had to let them go.
Uh-oh. We have company ...

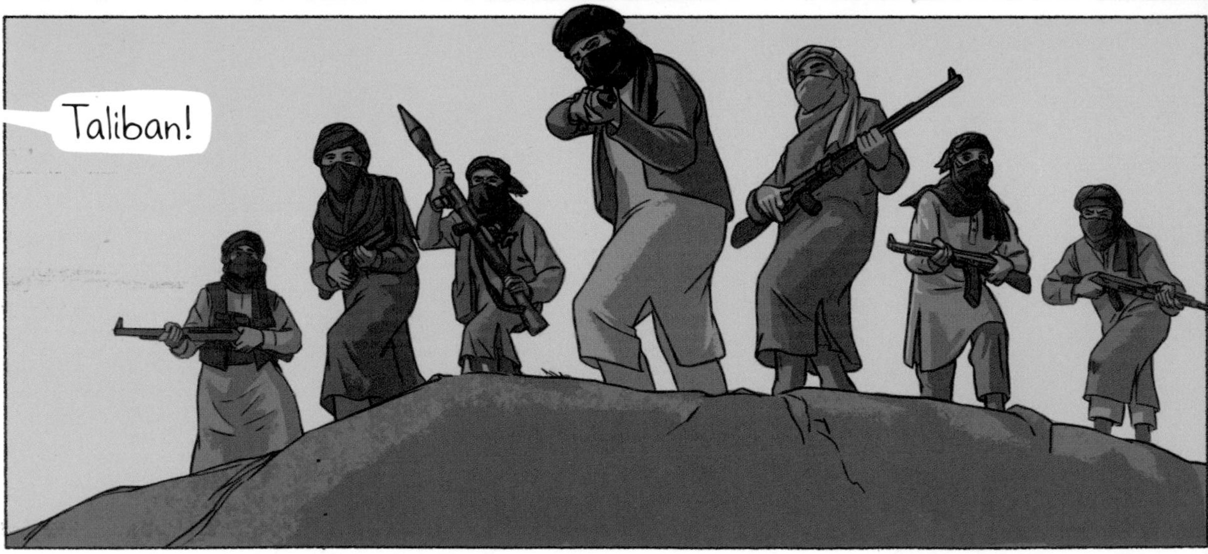
Taliban!

A fierce firefight erupted between the SEALs and about 100 Taliban warriors. SEALs Matt Axelson, Danny Dietz, and Mike Murphy were killed.

Only Marcus Luttrell survived the brutal struggle. He was alive, but he had lost his food, water, phone, and helmet in the battle.

The next day, Luttrell tried to make his way through the mountains, but the Taliban followed close behind.

They're still on my trail. I need to lose them.

Meanwhile, news broadcasts around the world began reporting that a mission to rescue the SEALs had failed. Taliban fighters shot down a U.S. helicopter, killing all 16 Americans aboard.

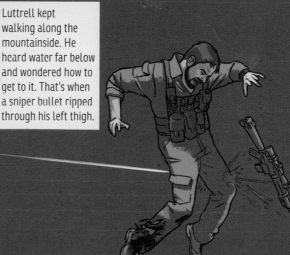

Luttrell kept walking along the mountainside. He heard water far below and wondered how to get to it. That's when a sniper bullet ripped through his left thigh.

The impact of the bullet knocked Luttrell backward down the steep mountain. By the time his enemies found him, Luttrell was ready.

SHRING!

Two more Taliban appeared, but Luttrell tossed a grenade at them.

Aaaaah!

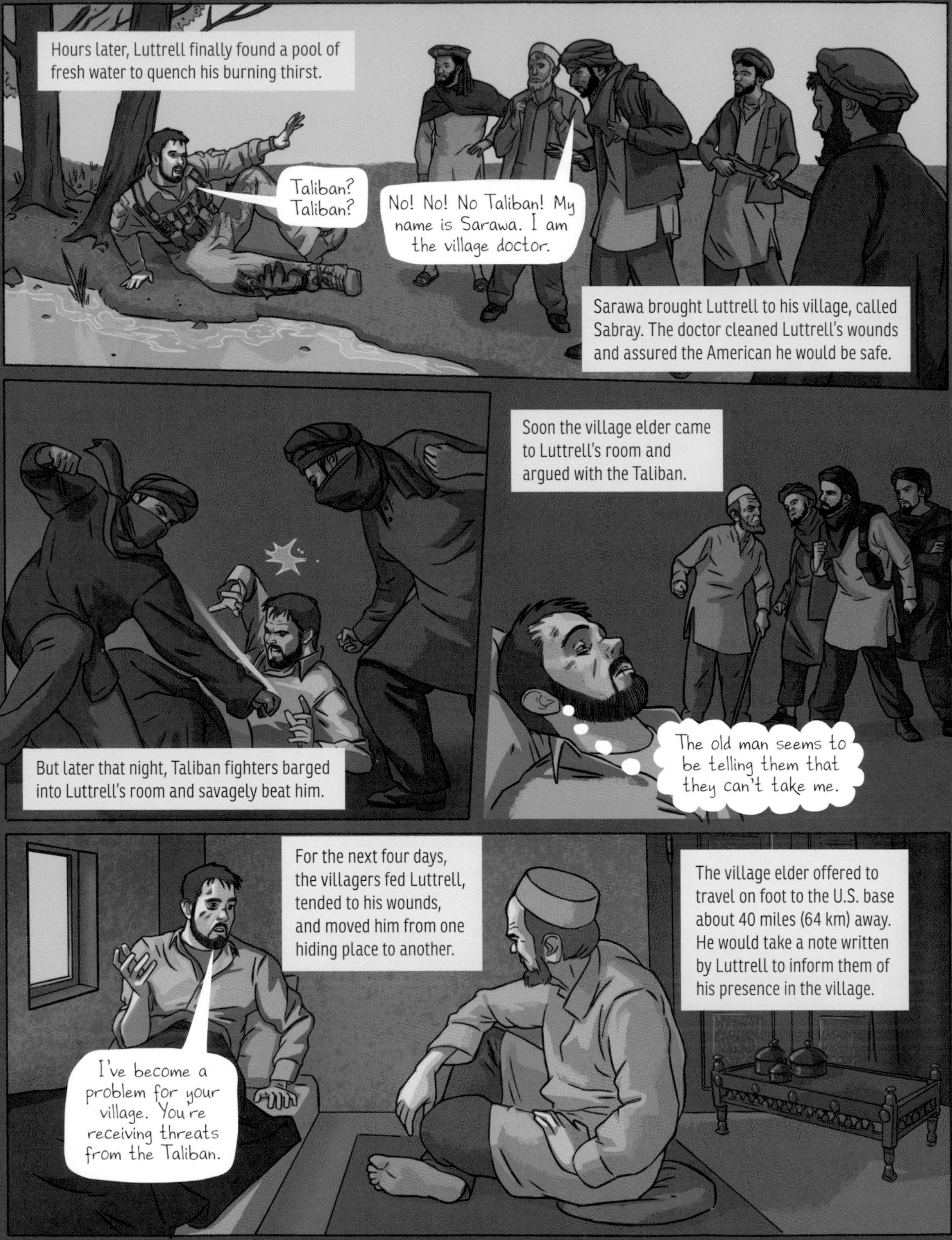
Hours later, Luttrell finally found a pool of fresh water to quench his burning thirst.
Taliban? Taliban?
No! No! No Taliban! My name is Sarawa. I am the village doctor.
Sarawa brought Luttrell to his village, called Sabray. The doctor cleaned Luttrell's wounds and assured the American he would be safe.
But later that night, Taliban fighters barged into Luttrell's room and savagely beat him.
Soon the village elder came to Luttrell's room and argued with the Taliban.
The old man seems to be telling them that they can't take me.
For the next four days, the villagers fed Luttrell, tended to his wounds, and moved him from one hiding place to another.
I've become a problem for your village. You're receiving threats from the Taliban.
The village elder offered to travel on foot to the U.S. base about 40 miles (64 km) away. He would take a note written by Luttrell to inform them of his presence in the village.

The U.S. military might believe one of us SEALs is still alive. I need to give them some kind of signal. Maybe they can pick up a radio emergency beacon from my transmitter.

With the note from the village elder and his beacon, the Americans pinpointed Luttrell's location.

Bombs from U.S. planes! They've found me!

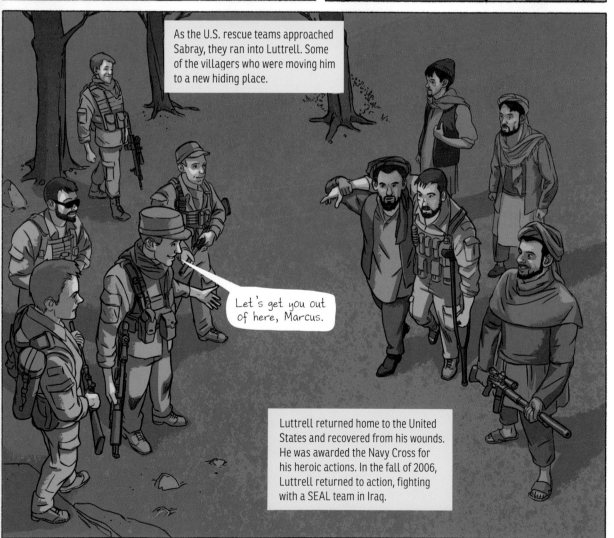

As the U.S. rescue teams approached Sabray, they ran into Luttrell. Some of the villagers who were moving him to a new hiding place.

Let's get you out of here, Marcus.

Luttrell returned home to the United States and recovered from his wounds. He was awarded the Navy Cross for his heroic actions. In the fall of 2006, Luttrell returned to action, fighting with a SEAL team in Iraq.

GLOSSARY

CONTAMINATED *(kuhn-TAM-uh-nay-tid)*—dirty or unfit for use

DEHYDRATED *(dee-HYE-dray-tid)*—not having enough water

DROPSY *(DROP-see)*—a condition in which watery fluids build up in the tissues of the body

FLANK *(FLANGK)*—the far left or right side of a group of soldiers

HYDRAULICS *(hye-DRAW-liks)*—a system powered by fluid forced through pipes or chambers

LOADMASTER *(lode-MAS-tur)*—a crew member on a military or civilian aircraft

MOBILE *(MOH-buhl)*—able to move or be moved easily

MORTAR *(MOR-tur)*—a short cannon that fires shells or rockets high in the air

SCURVY *(SKUR-vee)*—a deadly disease caused by a lack of vitamin C; scurvy produces swollen limbs, bleeding gums, and weakness

SHRAPNEL *(SHRAP-nuhl)*—pieces that have broken off from an explosive shell

TRIPOD *(TRYE-pahd)*—a stand with three legs that is used to steady a weapon, camera, or other piece of equipment

READ MORE

Hunter, Nick. *Military Survival.* Extreme Survival. Chicago: Raintree, 2011.

Nelson, Maria. *Heroes of the U.S. Marines.* Heroes of the U.S. Military. New York: Gareth Stevens, 2013.

Yomtov, Nel. *True Stories of World War I.* Stories of War. North Mankato, Minn.: Capstone Press, 2013.

INTERNET SITES

FactHound offers a safe, fun way to find Internet sites related to this book. All of the sites on FactHound have been researched by our staff.

Here's all you do:

Visit *www.facthound.com*

Type in this code: 9781491465714

Super-cool stuff! Check out projects, games and lots more at **www.capstonekids.com**

INDEX